What people have said about the first edition of this book –

From Amazon.com – Reader Comments
To the point! 2003 ★ ★ ★ ★
"This book does an excellent job of showing how to remove unwanted mineral excess from everyday foods. A great kitchen read for those who want instructions spelled out in as few a pages as possible".

An important self-help guide that was long overdue, 2003 ★ ★ ★ ★
"When kidneys fail, minerals build up in the blood. Living with this constant fear can mean the end of eating pleasure. Using the step-by-step instruction. for processing various food selections listed in this guide can reduce minerals in foods and help someone return to a more normal eating lifestyle".

From Barnes and Noble.com Reader Reviews
A reviewer: A kidney patient, 2004 ★ ★ ★ ★
"A Long Overdue Cookbook. Finally, a book that shows us how to remove mineral excess from our food so we can eat again!"

A reviewer: A participant in that ADA study, 2003 ★ ★ ★ ★
"Useful and to the point. This book was used in an ADA education study with ESRD patients. Very helpful to those who used it".

A reviewer, A renal person, 2003 ★ ★ ★ ★
"A GOOD GUIDE!
Simple, and easy to follow instructions for those of us who need to get phosphorus and potassium out of what we eat to stay healthy!"

A reviewer: Renal researcher, ★ ★ ★ ★
"Easy to read - easy to follow
This book is easy to read and follow - a real must when getting an important message like this across to the hundreds of thousands with kidney failure".

A reviewer: I am a renal patient, 2003 ★ ★ ★ ★
"Worth much more to me than the cost.
I was told to limit my phosphorus and potassium by my renal dietitian. This was hard because all foods have these minerals. But when I started processing my food according to the instructions in this book, my potassium sodium and phosphorus returned to normal!"

"An exciting project that can really help both patients and clinicians. "
Susan O. Smith, MS, RD
National Kidney Foundation Volunteer
Former Practicing Renal Dietitian
Product Specialist for Ortho-Biotech

AND…
For those who want to take control of their
dietary creatine –

More Bio-fuel
=
Less Bio-waste

Dietary Creatine Reduction Self-help
Guide for People with Kidney Impairment

Wendy Lou Jones, MS, BA

Also available through on-line bookstores across the Web!

Food – *Fuel* – Fitness

Healthy Living with Food Demineralization
2nd Edition

An EZ food preparation guide for lowering mineral intake

Including -

"A Word About"

Carbs
Fats
Protein *and more!*

Wendy Lou Jones, MS, BA

Forewords by Wendy Lou Jones and Beth McQuiston, MS, RD, LD

RK Books

Food - Fuel - Fitness

Healthy Living with Food Demineralization

2nd Edition

An EZ food preparation guide for lowering mineral intake

Royal Knight, Incorporated
At: RoyalKnightInfo@yahoo.com

This edition was produced for on-demand distribution
By **Lightning Source**

Originally published in paperback format by **SuperiorBooks.com, Inc.**
First Edition: March 2002
Softcover ISBN: 1931055580
Printed in the United States of America

Second Edition Published by
Royal Knight, Inc.

RK
Books
2006
Second Edition Softcover ISBN: 0-9777110-0-5
Printed in the United States of America

This book is dedicated to my mother, Maryann D. Jones, without whose complete support in every aspect of my writing projects, none of this would be possible.

When you can't raise the bridge, lower the river – *anyway you have to!*

W.L.J.

TABLE of CONTENTS

Foreword for the Second Edition

Food – *Fuel* – Fitness, is the second edition of **Healthy Living with Food Demineralization**, and is filled with an array of surprises for the reader. In addition to a streamlined format, and a new reader-friendly style, this edition is bursting with twice the number of delicious foods to tempt any appetite.

Far from being '*tasteless cardboard*', mineral reduced foods bring distinct subtle aromas and flavors to every meal, inviting creative embellishment with one's own secret blend of herbs and spices. **Food – *Fuel* – Fitness** offers a few recipes as 'idea starters', inviting the reader to use their own imagination in exploring creative low-mineral recipes.

The enhanced *A Word About* section addressed a few inconspicuous places minerals may be lurking, as well as the impact mineral reduction techniques have on carbohydrates, fats, protein, and amino acid compositions of selected foods. And for those who may be concerned about the flavor enhancing sodium phosphate **food additives** now found in many meats and poultry in the U.S.A, as well as in other countries, the impact on the meat's mineral level is discussed in this chapter, as well as in the respective meat section.

Finally, at the end of the book, you are cordially invited to share your own experiences – how mineral reducing your food has impacted your life and health – for inclusion in a possible *Third edition* of this book.

Wendy Lou Jones, MS, BA

Foreword for the First Edition

Wendy Lou Jones has researched, created, and written a revolutionary and landmark text allowing more flexibility and variety in food choices for dialysis patients. After several frustrating years of wondering how much potassium, phosphorus, and sodium can be removed by common household methods, her research has definitively ended this speculation.

Using the techniques outlined in this book, and working with the healthcare team, will give dialysis patients more flexibility to fit favorite foods into their diet. In addition to highlighting important food safety tips, much care and thought has been put into developing an easy to use, practical guide that can be used in conjunction with the National Renal Diet, as well as other educational tools. Perhaps of greatest importance, each food item has been tested for quality and taste after processing to ensure the demineralized food actually tastes great!

Particularly impressive is the sheer number of foods tested and reviewed. By following these carefully researched and effective techniques, dialysis patients can enjoy even more variety in their foods while eating healthful, flavorful meals.

This text is helpful for dialysis patients, caregivers and healthcare providers in customizing a diet plan to best meet the needs of the individual.

After many years of speculation, we finally have answers to which foods can be demineralized and exactly how to do it. This comprehensive and outstanding resource is sure to become a classic for dialysis patients and the healthcare team alike.

Beth McQuiston, MS, RD, LD

Web Pages

The Web page-links sited in this edition were checked for accuracy just before this edition went to press in 2006. Subsequent changes or alterations to either the links, or the web page data to which they originally pointed, is beyond the control of either the author or the publisher, and neither shall be held responsible for such alterations.

Acknowledgement

Some of the numerical demineralization data, appearing on the pages that follow, was reprinted by permission from the Journal of Renal Nutrition[13]

Royal Knight Inc., wishes to extend a special "thank you" to Dr. Jerry King, and his excellent staff at Midwest Laboratory, Inc., in Omaha Nebraska, for their food analytical work for this project.

The author would like to acknowledge Beth McQuiston, MS, RD, LD, and Susan O. Smith, MS, RD, for their editorial assistance and suggestions regarding the first edition.

Food – *Fuel* – Fitness

Healthy Living with Food Demineralization

2nd Edition

An EZ food preparation guide for lowering mineral intake

Introduction

Welcome to **Food - Fuel - Fitness,** the second edition of **Healthy Living with food Demineralization**. Any reader who has a copy of the first edition will find a large number of changes, including important mineral reduction data updates in this second edition.

Some of the data, concerning the ability of the food demineralization procedures to lower food phosphorus levels and subsequently patient serum phosphorus levels, was gleaned from a 2001- 2002 study. The food processing instructions in the original **<u>Healthy Living with Demineralization</u>** manual were tested in a small, cross-country, American Dietetics Association – Renal Practice Group (ADA-RPG) educational study. Individuals focused on demineralizing high phosphorus foods, and occasionally demineralized other foods in which the primary excess mineral was potassium. Data indicated modest potassium serum value decreases for 54% of participants in this study, however the most dramatic reductions occurred in serum phosphorous for 92% of respondents.

In a previous (unpublished) study, nutritional demineralization was shown to impact blood serum phosphorus, potassium, and sodium in both renal and control volunteers. The extent of the impact varies with the percentage of the individual's diet being demineralized. In individuals with a significant amount of residual kidney function remaining, it may be possible to reduce serum potassium and phosphorus to near, or within the recommended range, for these minerals when <u>absolutely</u> 100% of all foods eaten have been correctly mineral reduced.

Why Demineralize Food?

The information on food demineralization presented in this book is based on demineralization data from numerous studies conducted by the author.

The statistics are nothing short of grim.

Today, more than 20 millions, in the United States (approximately 60 million world-wide[14]), have some degree of chronic kidney disease placing them *'at risk'* for developing End Stage Renal Disease (ESRD). Despite advances in medical technology, each year thousands upon thousands of those with chronic kidney disease transition to ESRD and the need for renal replacement (primarily dialysis). As of 2005, the number of people undergoing some form of dialysis in the U.S. was estimated upwards at 380,000 - 400,000, with an annual increase in incident rate of approximately 5% - 7%. If this alarming trend continues, it has been projected that – by the year 2010, more than 650,000 will likely be on some form of dialysis, and by 2025, more than 2.2 million people will require renal support, just to stay alive [1-2].

Healthy kidneys perform many life-sustaining functions, some of which involve production of erythropoietin (EPO) for the creation of red blood cells, the elimination of wastes (urea, creatinine, etc.), and regulation of mineral levels [3 – 7]. Phosphorus, potassium, and sodium — abundant to various degrees in the foods we normally eat, are three of the most problematic food-related minerals to regulate when kidneys fail. As kidney function deteriorates, waste and mineral concentrations increase sharply. This may lead to nausea, electrolyte imbalance, and may contribute to malnutrition, high blood pressure (hypertension), fluid overload, and heart problems (cardiac congestion) [8].

This book was developed in order to allow kidney patients (especially those undergoing hemodialysis) to enjoy foods they are traditionally told to avoid. Simple food-processing instructions were developed to reduce minerals (demineralize) in food before it is eaten. By using these simple, easy to follow, demineralization instructions, the phosphorus, potassium, and sodium content of numerous fruits, vegetables, legumes, meats, flours, and even cheeses, can be reduced significantly. Demineralization can make many restricted, and even excluded, high potassium, phosphorus, and sodium foods permissible on a renal diet once again. By eating the majority of a total dietary selection demineralized, one should expect to see an improvement in their problematic phosphorus, potassium, and sodium blood (hematological) mineral values, and in their nutritional status.

Because certain water-soluble vitamins (B vitamins, vitamin C) minerals and iodine can also be removed during demineralization, it may be necessary to replace those losses with supplements. Tell your dietitian and physician that you have begun eating many of your foods mineral reduced, and ask to be checked for water-soluble vitamin, mineral and iodine deficiencies. Your doctor or dietitian may recommend a vitamin and mineral supplement made especially for your special condition and needs.

Note – Demineralizing your food, according to the procedures described herein, will cause large losses of nutritional potassium and sodium. If you are performing peritoneal dialysis, talk to your doctor or renal dietitian about the amount of potassium/sodium loss that is right for you, before you begin demineralizing your food.

How to use this book

Each food item is presented with a chart that shows at a glance:

1. The food selection: **HAMBURGER**

2. Whether it is dried, canned, fresh, etc: **(Beef – fresh)**

3. The original mineral concentration per 100 grams (about 3 ½ ounces) of the food material,

before demineralization, for one or more of the target minerals:

Na = sodium

K = potassium

P = phosphorus

are displayed under a symbol to indicate, at a glance, whether the mineral level for that entry

is: **(High)**   **(Medium)**   **(Low)**

                          X mg   **X mg**   **X mg**

4. The demineralization instructions follow: **'How to Mineral Reduce this Food'**

5. The **'Optimal Processing Time'** for the food selection is given; (e.g., **'X Minutes'**)

6. **'Approximate mineral concentration per 100 grams after demineralization'** is shown

under a second symbol at the bottom of the page,

7. Along with, **'Approximate mineral reduction potential after demineralization'** (**X%**)

8. **'Tips and/or Recipe Ideas'** follow on the opposing page,

It should be noted that there is no single 'standard' mineral concentration for any food. The original mineral content of any natural (unprocessed) food depends largely upon a number of uncontrollable factors (e.g., variety, stage of maturity, soil type, etc.). Depending upon the dietary source referenced, 100-grams of edible tomato flesh has been reported to contain the following concentrations of potassium:

Potassium concentration reported in 100 mg of tomato flesh from various nutritional references.

208 mg[1], 244 mg[2], 207 mg[3], 240 mg[4], 243 mg[5], 222 mg[6]

1. Jones WL. Demineralization of a Wide Variety of Foods for the Renal Patient. **Journal of Renal Nutrition**, JRN April 2001; 11(2): 90-96
2. Sodium and potassium content of foods, 100 gm, edible portion, In, **Mosby's Medical & Nursing Dictionary**, Urdang L and Swallow HH, (Eds), 1983, pp 1291.
3. Nutritive value of Foods, In, **Taber's Cyclopedic Medical Dictionary**, 16th ed. Davis FA (Ed), 1989, pp 2198.
4. Ashley R. and Duggal H., **Dictionary of Nutrition**, Published by Pocket Books, 1975 pp 234.
5. Pennington JAT, Wilkening VL. Final regulations for the nutritional labeling of raw fruits, vegetables, and fish. **Journal of the American Dietetic Association**, 1997;(97): 1299-1305.
6. Vegetables, Vegetable Products & Vegetable Salads (page 317), In, **Bowes & Church's Food Values of Portions Commonly Used**, 16th ed. Pennington, JAT (Ed), 1994.

Therefore, all mineral values sited in this book should be viewed as the mineral concentration *only* for the food sample that was tested. The 100-gram tomato that you demineralize may have slightly more or less potassium than is listed in this, *or any other*, nutritional guide. However, regardless of your tomato's initial mineral concentration, if you are carrying out the demineralization procedure <u>exactly</u> as described for tomatoes, you can reasonably expect the percent of potassium, that will be lost during the demineralization time, to approximate that shown in this book.

Words to Know

The following words will be used in relation to mineral content, mineral control, and the mineral reduction (demineralization) processes described in this book.

Demineralization

The removal of minerals from a substance. In this book, demineralization is accomplished exposing a food selection to water at various temperatures for various time periods. For kidney patients who often have phosphorus, potassium and sodium restrictions, this process helps fit a greater variety of foods into their diet.

Gram (g)

A unit of weight. A 100-gram sample is *approximately* equal to 3 ½ ounces, or a standard serving size for most foods.

'>' (*Greater than*) - When this symbol appears before a number (e.g. >10 mg or >10%) it means that the value is *greater than* the number shown, but an exact number could not be given for whatever reason.

K – A shorthand chemical symbol for potassium, used in this book.

'<' (*Less than*) - When this symbol appears before a number (e.g. <1 mg or <1%) it means that the value is *less than* the number shown, but an exact number could not be given for whatever reason.

Milligram (mg)

A unit of weight equaling 1/1000 of a gram. 1000 milligrams is equal to 1 gram. A serving size, as listed in this book, is 100 grams or approximately 3 ½ ounces.

Na - A shorthand chemical symbol for sodium, used in this book.

P – A shorthand chemical symbol for phosphorus, used *only* in this book.

Foods that Demineralize Poorly

While most foods tested processed well, some foods, because of excessive sliminess (mucilage - sticky gelatinous material), buoyancy, oiliness, poor structural integrity, or rapid loss of taste cannot be demineralized correctly. Below is a list of such foods that this author has found to be unacceptable for processing.

Dried Fruit

Endive

Many varieties of leaf lettuce

Mushrooms (raw only)

All nut meats

Okra (fresh only)

All seeds

All legume <u>butter</u> (peanuts, soy nuts, etc.)

Watermelon

All foods that are liquid at room temperature

Phosphorus, Potassium and Sodium

What is meant by Low, Medium, and High?

Regulation of internal mineral concentration is just one of many important life-sustaining functions kidneys must perform. As kidney function declines, maintaining the correct internal balance of **phosphorus, potassium**, and **sodium** becomes more difficult to regulate. Unfortunately, most raw, and *especially* processed, foods contain an overabundance of at least one or more of these minerals. Unrestricted consumption of such mineral laden foods can cause physiological mineral imbalance (especially excess in phosphorus, potassium and sodium), that can lead to potentially dangerous and even life threatening health problems. It is, therefore, important that you know the amount of phosphorus, potassium, and sodium, per serving, of the foods you are about to prepare, so that you can take steps to reduce them if they are too high for you. The following are definitions for low, medium and high mineral contents.

Phosphorus (P)

Neither the National Kidney Foundation, nor the American Dietetic Association has specified absolute low, medium, or high range guidelines for phosphorus per serving for kidney patients. With the exception of prepackaged foods, large concentrations of phosphorus are found primarily in meats, legumes/nuts, and dairy products. These foods supply essential protein and can not be eliminated from the diet. The National Kidney Foundation – Dialysis Outcomes Quality Initiative (NKF-DOQI) has made specific recommendations concerning protein – about 1.2 grams per kilogram of body weight/day for hemodialysis patients[9], and 1.2 – 1.3 grams per kilogram of body weight/day for chronic peritoneal dialysis (CPD).[10] Based on an average concentration of 14 – 17 mg of phosphorus per gram of protein, a general rule of thumb for the amount of phosphorus found in a diet which contains about 1.2 grams of protein/kg body weight, would reasonably be:

> For a 60kg person (132lb) = 1092 — 1326 mg of phosphorus/day;
> For a 70kg person (154lb) = 1274 —1547 mg phosphorus/day;
> For an 80kg person (176lb) = 1456 —1768 mg phosphorus/day.

Unfortunately, when little or no kidney function remains, many patients find it virtually impossible to maintain a normal, or even near normal, blood phosphorus level, consuming this amount of dietary phosphorus without substantial use of phosphate binders. The need for proper nutrition usually makes a low physiological phosphorus goal unattainable.

One of the many benefits to demineralizing food is that much lower nutritional phosphorus levels can be achieved without sacrificing needed protein. Using the demineralization procedures detailed in this book, this author has achieved a greater than 40% reduction for phosphorus in most beans, legumes, and meats tested.

Based on the nutritional phosphorus reduction potential achievable by using the demineralization procedures listed in this book, this author has calculated *prospective* low, medium, and high ranges for the food selections tested. It is understood that these ranges are **only** intended for use within the context of this book.

[a] ***Low***: 0 - 110 mg or less per serving

[b] ***Medium***: 111 - 200 mg per serving

High: 201 mg or more per serving

*The above calculations were based on a daily phosphorus limit of 1000 mg, distributed across 3 meals per day (with 2 or 3 phosphorus items per meal) in the following calculation:

[a] 110 mg of P per each 100 gram item x 3 items per meal x 3 meals/day
= less than 1000 mg of phosphorus/day (about 990 mg of P)

[b] 200 mg of P per each 100 gram item x 2 items per meal x 3 meals/day
= more than 1000 mg of phosphorus (about 1200 mg of P)

(To illustrate a point — performing a 30-minute demineralization procedure on beef hamburger will reduce the phosphorus content an *average* of more than 40%, placing it in the *low* phosphorus category, **according to this book**. An individual would *theoretically* have to consume more than1400 grams [about 50 ounces, or more then 3 lb.] of demineralized hamburger [containing roughly 325 - 350 grams of protein], in order to have consumed 1000 mg of phosphorus).

Potassium (K)

Existing guidelines for hemodialysis patients generally recommend limiting potassium ingestion (approximately 60 - 70 milliequivalents (mEq) or about 2,300 to 2,700 mg per day),[11] depending upon individualized medical restrictions. The following defined low, medium, and high values for potassium per serving are currently in use for **hemodialysis** patients:

> *Low:* 0 – 100 mg per serving
> *Medium:* 101 – 200 mg per serving
> *High:* 201 mg – or more per serving

Sodium (Na)

Currently, hemodialysis patients are usually told to limit sodium intake to between 2 – 3 grams or 2000 – 3000 mg per day, depending upon individualized medical restrictions. The government nutrition labeling guidelines[12] specify that food with less than:

 5 mg of sodium per serving can be labeled "sodium-free",

35 mg or less per serving - "very-low-sodium",

less than 140 mg of sodium per serving - "low-sodium".

The National Renal Diet patient education and meal planning booklets have labeled any foods, with more than 250 mg of sodium, with a saltshaker symbol *suggesting* "high sodium". While professional renal nutrition guidelines for sodium, in use today, do not state defined low or medium classifications for this mineral, using the government nutrition labeling guidelines and the National Renal Diet patient education information, this author has ascribed *prospective* low, medium, and high *ranges.* It is understood that these ranges are intended for use **only** within the context of this book

   Low: 0 – 140 mg per serving

   Medium: 141 – 249 mg per serving

   High: 250 mg or more per serving

Some of the numerical demineralization data, appearing on the pages that follow, was reprinted by permission from the Journal of Renal Nutrition[13]

Further Reading

1. Osinski M, and Wish J. Physician Workforce: Coming up short. Nephrology News and Issues. March 2005: 58-59, 64.

2. Jones CA, McQuillan GM, Kusek JW, et al. Serum creatinine levels in the U.S. Population: Third National Health and Nutrition Exam Survey. Am. J. Kid. Dis. 1999: 34(suppl. 1):540-550.

3. Eschbach JW. The anemia of chronic renal failure. Kidney Int. 1989: 35:134-148.

4. Schuster VL, Seldin DW: Renal clearance, in Seldin DW, Giebisch G (eds): The Kidney, vol I: Physiology and Pathophysiology. New York, NY, Ravin, 1985: pp 365- 395.

5. Gillin AG, Sands JM: Urea transport in the kidney. Semin Nephrol 1993: 13:146-154.

6. Kunis CL, Charney AN: Potassium and renal failure. Compr Ther 1981: 7(3):29-33.

7. Kaji D, Thomas K: Na+ -K+ pump in chronic renal failure. Am J Physiol 1987: 252(5 Pt); F785-793.

8. Maiorca R, Brunori G, Zubani R, et al: Predictive value of dialysis adequacy and nutritional indices for mortality and morbidity in CAPD and HD patients. A longitudinal study. Nephrol Dial Transplant 1995: 10; 2295-2305.

9. Kidney Disease Outcome Quality Initiative (DOQI). Management of Protein and Energy Intake. Dietary Protein Intake (DPI) in Maintenance Hemodialysis (MHD). AJKD 2000: 35(No.6 – suppl. 2):S40-41.

10 Kidney Disease Outcome Quality Initiative (DOQI). Management of Protein and Energy Intake. Dietary Protein Intake (DPI) for Chronic Peritoneal Dialysis (CPD). AJKD 2000: 35(No.6 – suppl. 2):S42-43.

11 Ahmed KJ, Kopple JD: Nutrition in Maintenance Hemodialysis Patients. Factors Altering Nutrient Requirements in Maintenance Hemodialysis Patients, in Kopple JD, Massry SG (eds): Nutritional Management of Renal Disease. Williams and Wilkins, Baltimore, Maryland, 1997: pp 563-600.

12 Anonymous. Understanding Food Labels. ADA (food label pamphlet) 1998.

13 Jones, WL. Demineralization of a Wide Variety of Foods for the Renal Patient. J Ren Nutr 2001: 11(2): 90-96.

14. Anonymous. Cardiovascular Risk Factors Could Indicate Kidney Problems. Reported in Doctors Guide – Personal Edition (Web Based Journal). [Original source] Blackwell Publishing Ltd., May 19th, 2005.

Food Safety

Improper food handling can lead to food poisoning!

It is absolutely essential that all food handling, processing, and storage procedures be carried out with **clean** hands, on a **clean** surface, using **clean** food preparation utensils. Using the procedures listed, this author has safely demineralized various freshly ground and whole meats for consumption by control/renal volunteers.

Check **all** foods, especially canned goods and meats, for any 'off' smell, color, or abnormal appearance. Discard any outdated foods without tasting them. Wash and peel, or otherwise clean, all fruits, vegetables, beans and legumes before beginning the demineralization process. Be sure to store all food materials, undergoing extended cold water demineralization, **in the refrigerator.**

Be *especially* careful with meats. Ground or processed meat may contain more bacteria than a solid chunk of meat. Some of the meats, listed in this guide, are subjected to a 30 minute warm water (approximately 100°F) demineralization. Exposing meat to warm water will cause bacteria to multiply; so, before beginning any demineralization procedure, check the meat you are intending to demineralize and be absolutely certain that it is not already spoiled (when in doubt – throw it out!). Be sure to discard any meat that has reached the expiration date.

Be sure to defrost frozen meat in the refrigerator, **not on the counter at room temperature!** Improperly defrosted meat can lead to food poisoning.

Store all demineralized foods, not immediately cooked or eaten, in the refrigerator. Demineralized foods spoil very quickly. Be sure to eat, cook, or freeze all demineralized foods within 24 hours (this author has experienced no problems leaving demineralized cheese, pineapple, tangerines, and olives in the refrigerator for 48 hours). Freezing will prevent spoilage, allowing you to process large batches of food and keep it for later use.

CHEESE

Cheese – Take Note

When using cheese it is important to remember that cheese, in general, is a high phosphorus and sodium food. Food demineralization will have the greatest impact on sodium because it is added during the processing of cheese.

Of all the cheeses tested by this author, goat cheese crumbles had the lowest starting phosphorus level, and after demineralization, finished with an overall lower mineral level.

Cheese Tested

American Processed Cheese (sheets)

Cheddar Cheese (large curds – dry)

Goat Cheese (crumbles)

Swiss Cheese (slices)

AMERICAN PROCESSED CHEESE

(Processed cheese - sheets)

Approximate mineral concentration per 100 grams (about 5 sheets) **before** demineralizing:

STOP	STOP	STOP
K 247 mg	P 471 mg	Na 1054 mg

How to Mineral Reduce this Food

Author's note - An average serving is one or two sheets of cheese. However, for purposes of this book, all foods and their respective test mineral values, are listed per 100-gram quantity – for American Processes (sheet) cheese, that was approximately 5 sheets. One sheet of American Processed cheese can reasonably be expected to have approximately 20% of the above listed mineral content

Step one: Unwrap the desired number of cheese slices. If cheese is packaged as a block, slice cheese thinly (1/8" or less in thickness). This process may be made easier if the block of cheese is placed in the freezer until it become slightly "stiff" (not frozen).

Step two: Place your cheese in a *minimum* of 4 times the volume of warm (approximately 100ºF) tap water (one-quart minimum for approximately 100 grams of cheese). Allow cheese to set on the counter for 30 minutes. Cheese will settle and tend to adhere to the bottom of the container – the water will become "milky" and a greasy skim will form on the surface – this is normal. Cheese should remain stuck to the bowl.

Step three: Drain water, now scrape or roll the soft cheese onto a couple of paper towels. After the excess moisture has been removed, scrape or roll the cheese off of the towels and into a container and allow it to harden in the refrigerator. Cheddar and American Processed cheese will taste very mild after processing

Optimal Processing Time: 30 Minutes*

Approximate mineral concentration per 100 grams (about 3 ½ ounces) **after** demineralizing:

GO	STOP	STOP
K 90 mg	P 364 mg	Na 574 mg

Approximate mineral reduction potential **after** demineralizing:

64%	23%	45%

Tips and Recipe Ideas for: American Processed Cheese

* Cheese can be demineralized for 1 hour. This time period produces a cheese with a lower mineral value, but cheese lost in the water will be more pronounced. A one-hour mineral reduction treatment will produce a <u>very</u> mild tasting final product. Extending the demineralization time beyond 1 hour leaves the final product tasteless.

Remember to remove as much of the moisture, before storing, as possible. Cheese will loose a great deal of moisture in 5 to 7 minutes by setting undisturbed on paper towels. Cheese can then be carefully scraped, or rolled, into a container for storage. The final product will resemble a tub cheese. Taste is mild.

Demineralized cheese will spoil (sour) quickly. Be sure to keep demineralized cheese in the refrigerator and use within a 48 hours. This author has never attempted to keep demineralized cheese longer than three (3) days.

Tub Cheese 'Swirl'

Demineralized American processed cheese makes a great 'tub' cheese – as a dip for vegies or a topping for your demineralized potatoes or bread spread. Here's how its done:

Warm your demineralized cheese until it can easily be stirred with a spoon or fork;

To every 1 cup of cheese, mix 1-2 TBS of mayonnaise, and a little sugar (optional) to taste;

Add a 1-2 TSP of demineralized and grated onion (to taste);

Add 1 TBS of demineralized green (or red) pepper puree (previously made in a blender), or finely chopped pimento;

Now swirl the pepper puree (or pimento) creatively through the mix – chill and serve.

CHEDDAR CHEESE
(Shredded)

Approximate mineral concentration per 100 grams (about 3 ½ ounces) **before** demineralizing:

GO   STOP   STOP

K 60 mg   **P** 400 mg   **Na** 511 mg

How to Mineral Reduce this Food

Step one: Measure out the desired amount of cheese.

Step two: Place your cheese in a *minimum* of 4 times the volume of warm (approximately 100°F) tap water (one-quart minimum for approximately 100 grams of cheese). Allow cheese to set on the counter for 30 minutes. Cheese will become very soft, settle to the bottom of the container and tend to adhere – water will become "milky" and a greasy skim will form on the surface – this is normal.

Step three: Drain water, scrape or roll the soft cheese onto a couple of paper towels. After the excess moisture has been removed, scrape or roll the cheese off of the towels and into a container. Allow cheese to harden in the refrigerator. Both Cheddar and American Processed cheeses will taste very mild after processing.

Optimal Processing Time: 30 Minutes*

Approximate mineral concentration per 100 grams (about 3 ½ ounces) **after** demineralizing:

GO   STOP   GO

K 9 mg   **P** 368 mg   **Na** 56 mg

Approximate mineral reduction potential **after** demineralizing:
85%   **8%**   **89%**

Tips: Cheddar Cheese

* This author has demineralized cheese for 1 hour, reducing the sodium 97% and potassium to below the detection limit (>99%). Cheese lost in the water is very pronounced at one hour. A one-hour mineral reduction treatment will produce a very mild tasting final product. Extending the demineralization time beyond 1 hour leaves the final product tasteless.

Remember to remove as much of the moisture before storing as possible. Cheese will loose a great deal of moisture in 5 to 7 minutes by just setting undisturbed on paper towels. Cheese can then be carefully scraped, or rolled, into a container for storage. The final product will resemble a tub cheese. Taste is mild.

Demineralized cheese will spoil (sour) quickly. Be sure to keep demineralized cheese in the refrigerator and use within 48 hours. This author has never attempted to keep demineralized cheese longer than three (3) days.

Demineralized cheddar cheese is great over demineralized potatoes, bread, and in sandwiches. Use your imagination – the uses for demineralized cheddar cheese are virtually limitless!

COTTAGE CHEESE
(Large curds - dry)

Approximate mineral concentration per 100 grams (about 3 ½ ounces) **before** demineralizing:

CAUTION   CAUTION   STOP
K 106 mg   P 170 mg   Na 316 mg

How to Mineral Reduce this Food

Step one: Measure out the desired amount of cottage cheese to mineral reduce.

Step two: Place your cheese in a **minimum** of 4 times the volume of warm (approximately 100ºF) tap water (one-quart minimum for approximately 100 grams of cottage cheese). Allow cheese to set undisturbed on the counter for 30 minutes.

Step three: Drain cottage cheese in a sieve. Now place cottage cheese on a couple of paper towels to remove the maximum amount of moisture.

Optimal Processing Time: 30 Minutes

Approximate mineral concentration per 100 grams (about 3 ½ ounces) **after** demineralizing:

GO   CAUTION   CAUTION

K 48 mg   P <170* mg   Na 145 mg

Approximate mineral reduction potential **after** demineralizing:

55%   *(less than) 1%   54%

Tips and Recipe Ideas for: Cottage Cheese

Demineralized cottage cheese will spoil (sour) quickly. Be sure to keep mineral reduced cottage cheese in the refrigerator and use within 48 hours.

'Snow on the Mountain' fruit topping

Here's a cool idea for your low-fat chilled deserts using demineralized kiwi, cantaloupe, apple, and of course, cottage cheese.

Sliver ½ cup of each of the above fruits (alternately, the fruits can be pureed in a blender); Spoon fruit mixture into a small cup, then squirt a small dollop of honey (optional) on the top; Add 1 TBS of cottage cheese to the top of the mix and press gently to 'anchor' it; Now chill briefly, and serve. (Note - apple may 'brown' slightly)

GOAT CHEESE
(Crumbles)

Approximate mineral concentration per 100 grams (about 3 ½ ounces) **before** demineralizing:

GO   CAUTION   STOP

K 41 mg   **P 166 mg**   **Na 267 mg**

How to Mineral Reduce this Food

Step one: Measure out the desired amount of cheese to mineral reduce.

Step two: Place your cheese in a ***minimum*** of 4 times the volume of warm (approximately 100°F) tap water (one-quart minimum for approximately 100 grams of cheese). Let cheese settle to the bottom of the bowl. Allow cheese to set on the counter for 30 minutes.

Step three: Drain crumbles in a sieve. Now place the goat cheese on a couple of paper towels to remove the maximum amount of moisture.

Optimal Processing Time: 30 Minutes

Approximate mineral concentration per 100 grams (about 3 ½ ounces) **after** demineralizing:

GO   CAUTION   CAUTION

K 22 mg   **P 157 mg**   **Na 167 mg**

Approximate mineral reduction potential **after** demineralizing:
46%   **5%**   **37%**

Tips: Goat Cheese

Normally strong tasting goat cheese becomes much milder and less salty tasting after demineralizing.

Remember that any demineralized cheese will spoil quickly. Be sure to keep mineral reduced cheese in the refrigerator and use within 48 hours.

Goat cheese has its own distinct flavor. Experiment with different ideas for its use. Many people find the flavor satisfying to their taste buds.

SWISS CHEESE
(Slices)

Approximate mineral concentration per 100 grams (about 3 ½ ounces) **before** demineralizing:

K 83 mg   P 596 mg   Na 479 mg

How to Mineral Reduce this Food

Step one: Unwrap the desired number of cheese slices. If your Swiss cheese is packaged as a block, slice the cheese thinly (1/8" or less in thickness).

Step two: Place your cheese in a *minimum* of 4 times the volume of warm (approximately 100°F) tap water (one-quart minimum for approximately 100 grams of cheese). Let cheese settle to the bottom of the bowl. Allow cheese to set on the counter for 30 minutes – water will become "milky" and a greasy skim will form on the surface – this is normal

Step three: Drain water and scrape cheese onto a couple of paper towels to remove the maximum amount of moisture before serving or refrigerating.

Optimal Processing Time: 30 Minutes

Approximate mineral concentration per 100 grams (about 3 ½ ounces) **after** demineralizing:

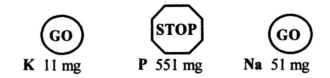

K 11 mg   P 551 mg   Na 51 mg

Approximate mineral reduction potential **after** demineralizing:
87%   8%   89%

Tips and Recipe Ideas for: Swiss Cheese

Extending the demineralization time to 1 hour leaves this cheese tasteless.

Remember that any demineralized cheese will spoil quickly. Be sure to keep mineral reduced cheese in the refrigerator and use within 48 hours.

Swiss Cheese and apple - "White Water" snack

The uses for demineralized Swiss cheese are virtually endless. Here is a creative and simple little snack you can try.

Spread no-trans-fatty acid margarine onto the face of lightly (or darkly – if you prefer) toasted bread;
Slice or dice demineralized apples in rows, on top;
Warm your demineralized Swiss cheese carefully in a microwave, then 'string' it up and down the rows of sliced or diced apples – serve warm (If necessary, re-warm before serving).

FRUITS

Fruits – Take Note

Fruits are not high in phosphorus nor in sodium unless it has been added during processing, as is the case in olives. In general fruits, even the potassium packed banana, respond very well to demineralization.

Fruits Tested

Apple (Fuji)

Avocado

Banana

Cantaloupe

Grapefruit

Kiwi

Olives

Tangerine

APPLE
(Fresh – *Fuji Apple*)

Approximate mineral concentration per 100 grams (about 3 ½ ounces) **before** demineralizing:

K 86 mg

How to Mineral Reduce this Food

Author's note - Apples are generally not considered a high potassium fruit, however, if you are planning to use many apples in a recipe, you may want to reducing the potassium content of your apples.

Step one: Wash or peel apples to remove any residual insecticide, dirt, and inedible external materials. Using a kitchen slicer, or knife, cut into slices of ¼ inch thickness or less and remove the seeds. Rinse all peeled fruits for 10 – 15 seconds under warm tap water (approximately100°F).

Step two: Place fruit slices in a *minimum* of 4 times its volume (or one-quart minimum) of warm tap water (approximately100°F), stir for 15 – 20 seconds, and allow food to set for one hour on the counter.

Step three: Drain water by pouring fruit slices into a sieve. If the apples are going to be used in a recipe which call for 'dry' fruit, place slices on one or more paper towels to remove the maximum amount of water.

Optimal Processing Time: 60 Minutes

Approximate mineral concentration per 100 grams (about 3 ½ ounces) **after** demineralizing:

K 57 mg

Approximate mineral reduction potential **after** demineralizing:
34%

Tips and Recipe Ideas for: Apples

Use demineralized apples anywhere you would normally use apples. Two old standbys immediately come to mind: Apple pie and applesauce. Demineralized apples are a little milder than non-mineral reduced apples, so if you are looking for 'zip' you may have to add a bit more sweetener to your recipe (let your taste buds be the judge).

Another use for demineralized apples, this time with a seasonal twist, is apple garnished demineralized pork, or demineralized turkey meat. Simply layer the demineralized fruit into the cooking bag and on top of the meat and you' re ready to go.

AVACADO
(Fresh)

Approximate mineral concentration per 100 grams (about 1/3 of an 8-oz. avocado) **before** demineralizing:

CAUTION

K 197 mg

How to Mineral Reduce this Food

Step one: Peel avocado. Using a kitchen knife cut fruit in half and remove the seed. Now cut fruit into slices of ¼ inch thickness or less. Rinse briefly under **cold** tap water.

Step two: Place fruit slices in a *minimum* of 4 times its volume (or one-quart minimum) of **cold** tap water, stir *gently* for 5 – 10 seconds to distribute the slices in the water. Now allow food to set for one hour in the refrigerator. At the end of the first hour, drain water *slowly* – slices are fragile – do not let them fall out of the bowl. Refill with **cold** tap water and return to the refrigerator for a second hour.

Step three: At the end of the second hour, once again drain water *slowly.* Tip fruit slices out of the bowl and onto a paper towel to remove the maximum amount of moisture.

Optimal Processing Time: 2 Hours

Approximate mineral concentration per 100 grams **after** demineralizing:

CAUTION

K 116 mg

Approximate mineral reduction potential **after** demineralizing:
41%

Tips for: Avocado

Never subject avocado slices to warm or hot water as this will cause the fruit to brown rapidly.

Avocados are classed as high potassium fruit. However potassium content can vary depending upon their origin and the degree of ripeness. The average potassium load for an avocado (8 oz - whole, with seed) is estimated at over 1000mg*.

Research conducted by this author suggests that a maximum potassium reduction of 40 - 41% can be achievable in the allotted time. Theoretically, this *could* reduce the potassium load of a 1000 mg (potassium content) avocado to approximately 450mg of potassium. Data suggests that a longer demineralization period will reduce the potassium load further, but taste is sacrificed after 2 hours.

Always treat slices of this fruit **very** gently. Slices can be damaged and will break up very easily during handling. The avocado slices will feel slippery during and after miner reduction. This is normal.

Demineralized fruit will not keep well. Always keep demineralized fruit in the refrigerator. Use within 24 hours.

Remember, since demineralized avocado can be easily fragmented or mashed, why not take advantage of this and top your salad with it.

* From: Nutritive Value of Food, Tabor Cyclopedia Medical Dictionary, 16th edition

BANANA
(Fresh)

Approximate mineral concentration per 100 grams (a 6" unpeeled banana is approximately 100 grams peeled, or about 3 ½ ounces) **before** demineralizing:

K 351 mg

How to Mineral Reduce this Food

Step one: Peel the banana. Using a kitchen knife, cut fruit into slices of ¼ inch thickness or less (crosswise or lengthwise). Rinse briefly under **cold** tap water.

Step two: Place fruit slices in a *minimum* of 4 times its volume (or one-quart minimum) of **cold** tap water, stir *gently* for 5 – 10 seconds to distribute the slices in the water. Now allow food to set for one hour in the refrigerator. At the end of the first hour, drain water *slowly* – slices are fragile – do not let them fall out of the bowl. Refill with **cold** tap water and return to the refrigerator for a second hour.

Step three: At the end of the second hour, once again drain water *slowly.* If the banana is intended for a pudding, pie, or cereal use you do not need to remove any more moisture. Simply proceed to your recipe.

If you need to remove more moisture, slide fruit slices out of the bowl and onto a paper towel before use.

Optimal Processing Time: 2 Hours

Approximate mineral concentration per 100 grams (about 3 ½ ounces) **after** demineralizing:

K 180 mg

Approximate mineral reduction potential **after** demineralizing:
49%

Tips for: Banana

Never subject banana slices to warm or hot water as this will cause the fruit to 'brown' *very* rapidly!

Treat slices of this fruit gently. Slices can be damaged and will break up very easily during handling. The banana slices will feel slippery during and after demineralization. This is normal.

Bananas are classed as a "high potassium" fruit. However, individual banana potassium content varies, depending upon many factors. Bananas prepared for puddings, cereal, or baked treats (pie, bread, cake, etc.) should be demineralized. Data suggests that a longer demineralization period (>2 hrs.) will reduce the potassium load much further, but taste is sacrificed after 2 hours.

Demineralized fruit will not keep well. You must use this fruit immediately.

CANTALOUPE
(Fresh)

Approximate mineral concentration per 100 grams (about 3 ½ ounces) **before** demineralizing:

K 229 mg

How to Mineral Reduce this Food

Step one: Rinse and peel the cantaloupe. Using a kitchen knife, open cantaloupe and remove the seeds, then rinse the inside. Slice a portion of the cantaloupe (which you intend to use today) into ¼ inch thickness, or less. Rinse slices for 10 to 15 seconds under warm tap water (approximately100°F).

Step two: Place fruit slices in a *minimum* of 4 times its volume (or one-quart minimum) of warm tap water (approximately100°F), stir for 5 – 10 seconds to distribute slices then, allow food to set for one hour on the counter. At the end of the first hour, drain water into a sieve, refill with **cold** tap water and place in the refrigerator for a second hour.

Step three: Drain water by pouring fruit slices slowly into a sieve.

Optimal Processing Time: 2 Hours

Approximate mineral concentration per 100 grams (about 3 ½ ounces) **after** demineralizing:

K 111 mg

Approximate mineral reduction potential **after** demineralizing:
52%

Tips for: Cantaloupe

If fruit will not be used immediately, place demineralized slices on several paper towels to remove excess liquid, then remove and store in a plastic container in the refrigerator. Sliced fruit is perishable, and is always best used within 24 hours. Demineralized fruit slices will expel excess water while setting in the storage container overnight. It is normal to see liquid in the bottom of the container by the next day. Discard liquid and consume the fruit.

Remember that mineral reduced fruit does not keep well. Always keep uneaten demineralized fruit in the refrigerator. Use within 24 hours or discard.

Cantaloupe makes a great additive to any cold salad, fruit cup, or stand-alone desert.

GRAPEFRUIT
(Fresh)

Approximate mineral concentration per 100 grams (about ¼ of a 1lb fruit) **before** demineralizing:

K 140 mg

How to Mineral Reduce this Food

Step one: Rinse and peel the grapefruit. Divide into sections and remove each section's white outer membrane, exposing the juice pouches. Remove the seeds. Rinse sections for 10 – 15 seconds under warm tap water (approximately100°F).

Step two: Place fruit slices in a *minimum* of 4 times its volume (or one-quart minimum) of warm tap water (approximately100°F), stir for 5 – 10 seconds, allow food to set for one hour on the counter.

Step three: Drain water by pouring fruit into a sieve.

Optimal Processing Time: 60 Minutes

Approximate mineral concentration per 100 grams (about 3 ½ ounces) **after** demineralizing:

K 77 mg

Approximate mineral reduction potential **after** demineralizing:
45%

Tips for: Grapefruit

Demineralized fruit slices will expel excess water while setting in the storage container overnight. It is normal to see liquid in the bottom of the container the next day. Discard liquid and consume the fruit.

Remember that mineral reduced fruit does not keep well. Always keep uneaten demineralized fruit in the refrigerator. Use within 24 hours or discard.

Special Note – Read your medication bottles and ask your pharmacist!

Some medications caution you not to eat grapefruit, or drink the juice, when taking a certain medication. This is because grapefruit juice is metabolized by the same enzyme in the liver that breaks down many commonly prescribed medications. More than 50 medications, including some used to treat high cholesterol, depression, high blood pressure, cancer, pain, impotence, and allergies, and yes – even birth control pills, should not be taken with (or near) grapefruit juice. If you are taking any medication, always remember to ask your pharmacist specifically if grapefruit juice is allowed.

KIWI
(Fresh)

Approximate mineral concentration per 100 grams (about 3 ½ ounces) **before** demineralizing:

K 246 mg

How to Mineral Reduce this Food

Step one: Rinse and peel the kiwi. Slice fruit into ¼ inch thickness, or less. Rinse sections for 10 – 15 seconds under warm tap water (approximately100°F).

Step two: Place fruit slices in a *minimum* of 4 times its volume (or one-quart minimum) of warm tap water (approximately100°F), stir for 5 – 10 seconds, allow food to set for one hour on the counter. At the end of the first hour, drain water by slowly pouring into a sieve, refill with cold tap water and place in the refrigerator for a second hour.

Step three: Finish by draining the final demineralization water slowly away from the fruit, and slipping the fruit onto a paper towel.

Optimal Processing Time: 2 Hours

Approximate mineral concentration per 100 grams (about 3 ½ ounces) **after** demineralizing:

K 127 mg

Approximate mineral reduction potential **after** demineralizing:
48%

Tips for: Kiwi

Kiwi is a 'tender' fruit. When changing the demineralizing bath, it is best not to let the fruit drop into the sieve or it could 'mush'.

Demineralized fruit slices will expel excess water while setting in the storage container overnight. It is normal to see liquid in the bottom of the container the next day. Discard liquid and consume the fruit.

Remember that mineral reduced fruit does not keep well. Always keep uneaten demineralized fruit in the refrigerator. Use within 24 hours or discard.

OLIVES

(Canned-pitted)

Approximate mineral concentration per 100 grams (about 3 ½ ounces) **before** demineralizing:

Na 560 mg

How to Mineral Reduce this Food

Step one: Drain and rinse the olives under warm tap water (approximately100°F).

Step two: Place olives in approximately 2 times its original volume of **cold** tap water. Stir for 5 – 10 seconds, allow food to set for 30 minutes on the counter.

Step three: Drain olives in a sieve. Refrigerate uneaten olives. Use with in 48 hours.

Optimal Processing Time: 30 Minutes

Approximate mineral concentration per 100 grams (about 3 ½ ounces) **after** demineralizing:

Na 383 mg

Approximate mineral reduction potential **after** demineralizing:
32%

Tips and Recipe Ideas for: Olives

Canned olives have a great deal of added sodium. While this author has found that it is possible to remove much more sodium by exposing olives to warm water for extended periods of time, taste suffers dramatically, rendering the final product unacceptable.

Kabobs, pizza topping, and salad

Mineral reduced (pitted) olives can be sliced or crushed and sprinkled on top of a salad or on a demineralized pizza (for the pizza recipe, see the instructions under the entry, "**Tips and Recipe Ideas: Beef Hamburger**"). They can also be spaced between sliced of mineral reduced cooked meats – Kabobs – and served warm from the microwave.

PINEAPPLE
(Canned-sliced)

Approximate mineral concentration per 100 grams (about 3 ½ ounces) **before** demineralizing:

K 124 mg

How to Mineral Reduce this Food

Step one: Open the can and drain pineapple into a sieve. Rinse pineapple rings under warm tap water (approximately100°F).

Step two: For every 20-ounce can of pineapple rings, use one-quart (minimum) of warm (approximately100°F) tap water. Add pineapple rings, stir for 5 – 10 seconds, allow food to set for one hour on the counter.

Step three: Drain pineapple in a sieve. Refrigerate uneaten rings. Use with in 24 hours for best flavor.

Optimal Processing Time: 60 Minutes

Approximate mineral concentration per 100 grams (about 3 ½ ounces) **after** demineralizing:

K 58 mg

Approximate mineral reduction potential **after** demineralizing:
53%

50

Tips and Recipe Ideas for: Pineapple

Demineralized fruit slices will expel excess water while setting in the storage container overnight. It is normal to see liquid in the bottom of the container the next day. Discard liquid and consume the fruit.

Tropical Smoothie

Smoothies are great for an afternoon beak, or even a breakfast starter, anytime of the year. Here is a suggestion.

To a blender, add ½ cup each of diced and demineralized pineapple and apple;
Add ½ cup of drained and rinsed peaches;
Add ½ to 1 cup of frozen blueberries (naturally low in potassium);
Add sweetener IF desired;
Also optional is a TSP of vanilla flavor (a complementary flavor to blueberries);
Add sufficient water to blend – blend on high until contents reach a nice smooth consistency.

This mix can be chilled briefly or eaten as is. Makes a great toping for hot bread or pancakes as well.

TANGERINE
(Canned - sliced)

Approximate mineral concentration per 100 grams (about 3 ½ ounces) **before** demineralizing:

K 215 mg

How to Mineral Reduce this Food

Step one: Open the can and drain tangerine slices in a sieve. Using a paring knife, remove the section membranes, and expose the juice pouches. Rinse under warm tap water (approximately100°F) briefly.

Step two: Use one-quart (minimum) of warm (approximately100°F) tap water per medium size can (about 10-16 ounces, add fruit, stir for 5 – 10 seconds, allow food to set for one hour on the counter. At the end of the first hour, drain water slowly into a sieve, refill with cold tap water and place in the refrigerator for a second hour.

Step three: Drain in a sieve. Refrigerate uneaten fruit. Use with in 24 hours.

Optimal Processing Time: 2 Hours

Approximate mineral concentration per 100 grams (about 3 ½ ounces) **after** demineralizing:

K 157 mg

Approximate mineral reduction potential **after** demineralizing:
27%

Tips for: Tangerines

This author has found that longer demineralization periods will further reduce the potassium load, however fruit will become tasteless.

Demineralized fruit slices will expel excess water while setting in the storage container overnight. It is normal to see liquid in the bottom of the container the next day. Discard liquid and consume the fruit.

Did you know -- tangerine fun facts

The Tangerine (botanical name *Citrus reticulata*) is a type of mandarin orange which originated from China. Its genus (Citrus) belongs to the Rutaceae or Rue family of which there are 140 genera and 1300 species distributed throughout the world. This name originated in Tangier Morocco, the port from which the first tangerines were shipped to Europe. Mandarins and satsumas are varieties of tangerine. Tangerine oil is pressed from the peel of ripe fruit and used in colognes and perfumes.

Read more At:
http://www.uga.edu/fruit/citrus.htm
http://thefoody.com/glossary/glossaryt.html

GRAIN

Grain – Take Note

Grain presents a 'double-whammy' of sorts in that they are generally high in both potassium and phosphorus. Grain's response to demineralization procedures is mixed. Though not listed in this book, canned wild rice will demineralize much faster then dry wild rice, straight from the bag.

Grain Tested

Barley

Brown Rice

Oatmeal

Wild Rice

BARLEY
(dry)

Approximate mineral concentration per 100 grams (about 2/3 cup) **before** demineralizing:

K 336 mg   P 228 mg

How to Mineral Reduce this Food

Step one: Measure out the desired amount of barley. Place up to one cup of barley in two quarts of *cold tap water and stir briefly to disperse. Let barley set on the counter for 30 minutes.

Step two: Pour barley quickly into a sieve. Place drained barley in the desire cook bowl and add the recommended amount of water and cook according to directions on the package.

Optimal Processing Time: Approximately 30 Minutes

Approximate mineral concentration per ever 100 grams (about 3 ½ ounces of the original ****dry barley**), after demineralizing:

CAUTION   STOP

K 161 mg   P 227 mg

Approximate mineral reduction potential **after** demineralizing:
52%   **<1%**

*NOTE - Barley, like oatmeal, can be placed in warm (approximately 100°F) water for up to one hour and it is reasonable to expect that the mineral level will be reduced further. However, there is no data available for this option in this edition.

NOTE – Barley, like oatmeal, will absorb some water during the demineralization process making it heavier. Your potential mineral load is always calculate on the bases of **<u>dry</u> weight. If you began the process with 100 grams (about 2/3 of a cup of barley) no matter what the final weight is, you still really have <u>*only*</u> 100 grams of (dry) barley.

BROWN RICE
(dry - short grain)

Approximate mineral concentration per 100 grams (about 2/3 cup) **before** demineralizing:

K 540 mg   P 375 mg

How to Mineral Reduce this Food

Step one: Measure out the desired amount of brown rice. Place in a sieve and rinse briefly under warm tap water (approximately 100°F). Allow rice to drain in a sieve while checking for stones and other non-food material.

Step two: Place brown rice in a **minimum** of 2 quarts (or 4 - 6 times the rice volume) of boiling water and stir intermittently, dispersing material completely. Boil for 10 -15 minutes, remove container from the heat and allow it to set for one hour.

Step three: Pour rice into a sieve – rinse once with tap water, and drain.

Optimal Processing Time: Approximately 75 Minutes **(total)**

Approximate mineral concentration per 100 grams (about 3 ½ ounces) **after** demineralizing:

K 46 mg   P 101 mg

Approximate mineral reduction potential **after** demineralizing:
91%   73%

Tips for: Brown Rice

Rice is an important food because it is a good starch, it tends to be non irritating to those with various intestinal maladies, and can be used in place of wheat flour for baking in various recipes.

Demineralized brown rice can be used as a side dish with vegetable, meats, and even as a dessert. For a tasty hot dish, try combining demineralized (and cooked) canned mushrooms, peas, and hamburger – add a dash of vegetable seasoning to bring out the flavor, or top with no-trans-fat margarine and serve.

OATMEAL
(Long cooking)

Approximate mineral concentration per 100 grams (about 3 ½ ounces – or, about one cup dry) **before** demineralizing:

K 387 mg   P 419 mg

How to Mineral Reduce this Food

Step one: Place one cup of dry rolled oats in a 2 quarts of warm tap water (approximately100°F).

Step two: Stir to dispersing the oats completely. Allow this to set for one hour on the counter.

Step three: Pour rolled oats carefully into a sieve to drain. Rolled oats are now hydrated (see the next page for post-processing cooking tips).

Author's note – this procedure can also be used on raw oat bran (there is no demineralization data for oat bran in this edition)

Optimal Processing Time: 60 Minutes

Approximate mineral concentration per 100 grams (about 3 ½ ounces) **after** demineralizing:

K 70 mg   P 147 mg

Approximate mineral reduction potential **after** demineralizing:
82%   **65%**

Tips for: Oatmeal

Oatmeal that has undergone mineral reduction processing is now hydrated. If you wish your oatmeal to have a stiffer consistency after cooking, you will have to reduce the amount of water normally used to cook with (author's suggestions – try reducing the amount of water used to cook the oats by only ½ cup initially).

WILD RICE
(dried)

Approximate mineral concentration per 100 grams (about 3 ½ ounces or about 1/2 - 3/4 cup) **before** demineralizing:

STOP   STOP

K 230 mg   P 270 mg

How to Mineral Reduce this Food

Author's note - Wild rice is very *difficult* to demineralize. The following instructions have given the best mineral reduction values in the shortest time. **Canned wild rice** is much easier to demineralize by using only hot water. You should reasonably expect lower final mineral values for demineralized canned wild rice. However, there is no data for **canned wild rice** option in this edition.

Step one: Measure out the desired amount of wild rice (1/2 to 1 cup are the easiest amounts to work with). Place in a sieve and rinse for at least 30 seconds under warm tap water (approximately 100°F). Allow rice to drain while checking for stones and other non-food material.

Step two: Place dry wild rice in a *minimum* of 2 quarts (or at least 4 – 6 times the rice volume when using more than one cup) of boiling water and stir to disperse. Allow water to come to a rolling boil once again, remove container from the heat and allow it to set for one hour. It is OK (but not necessary) to stir the wild rice intermittently.

Step three: After the first hour is finished, drain wild rice in a sieve.

Step four: Place swollen wild rice in a pressure cooker (*minimum* 4 cups of water per ½ cup of rice) and follow the cooking time and pressure instructions recommended by your guide. Drain after pressure cooking, rinse once in tap water, and finally drain.

Author's note – This author used an 8-quart programmable electric pressure cooker to process the wild rice, as follows: To ½ cup of wild rice (taken from step 3), 4 cups of water and 2 tablespoons of oil (to inhibit foaming) was added to the pressure cooker. The pressure was set at 15 lbs for 15 minutes. After pressure-cooking was complete, rice was drained, rinsed once in tap water, drained again, then served.

Optimal Processing Time: 1 Hour and 15 – 30 Minutes
(depending upon pressure cooking instructions)

Approximate mineral concentration per 100 grams (about 3 ½ ounces) **after** demineralizing:

GO   CAUTION

K <72 mg   P <142 mg

Approximate mineral reduction potential **after** demineralizing:
<69%   **<47%**

Tips for: Wild Rice

Compared to white or brown rice, wild rice is *very* difficult to demineralize.
In order to achieve the maximum mineral reduction, rice grains must split open and be exposed to the demineralization bath.

Wild rice can be used both seasonally and non-seasonally. It can be used as a stand-alone meal with other vegetables, in a salad, with a domestic or wild game meat, or sea food, as well as with fruit.

LEGUMES

Legumes -- Take Note

Legumes, like grain, are high in both potassium and phosphorus. Canned legumes tend to be lower in mineral value then their dry counterparts because they have been precooked, damaging the cells and allowing their mineral content to leak out.

Legumes Tested

Black beans

Butter beans

Garbonzo beans

Great Northern beans

Kidney beans

Lima beans

Peanuts

Red beans

Pinto beans

Soybeans

Soy grits

Tofu

BLACK BEANS

(Canned)

Approximate mineral concentration per 100 grams (about 3 ½ ounces) **before** demineralizing:

K 302mg   P 97 mg

How to Mineral Reduce this Food

Step one: Empty the contents of a can into a sieve and rinse for 15 to 30 seconds under warm tap water (approximately 100°F) then allow them to drain briefly.

Step two: Place beans in 4 times the volume (minimum of 1 quart per small can [about 1 cup] of beans) in warm tap water (approximately 100°F) stir vigorously for 15 – 20 seconds, and allow food to set for one hour on the counter.

Step three: After mineral reduction process has been completed, drain beans in a kitchen sieve.

Optimal Processing Time: 60 Minutes

Approximate mineral concentration per 100 grams (about 3 ½ ounces) **after** demineralizing:

K 144 mg   P 68 mg

Approximate mineral reduction potential **after** demineralizing:
52%   30%

See 'Tips and Recipe Ideas for: Multiple Beans' on page 75

BUTTER BEANS
(Canned)

Approximate mineral concentration per 100 grams (about 1/3 to 1/2 cup of drained beans) **before** demineralizing:

K 212 mg

P 50 mg

How to Mineral Reduce this Food

Step one: Empty the contents of a can into a sieve and rinse for 15 to 30 seconds under warm tap water (approximately 100°F) then allow them to drain briefly.

Author's note – To achieve the maximum mineral reduction, each bean *should* be cut at least once (preferably across the largest segment). This can be done quickly by pouring the beans onto a flat surface, using a long-blade bread knife, press down on groups of beans cutting them (approximately) in half. Return the cut beans to the sieve and rinse with warm tap water once again.

Step two: Place beans in 4 times the volume (minimum of 1 quart per small can [about 1 cup] of beans) in warm tap water (approximately 100°F) stir vigorously for 15 – 20 seconds, and allow food to set for one hour on the counter

Step three: After mineral reduction process has been completed, drain beans in a kitchen sieve.

Optimal Processing Time: 60 Minutes

Approximate mineral concentration per 100 grams (about 3 ½ ounces) **after** demineralizing:

GO

K 88 mg

GO

P 46 mg

Approximate mineral reduction potential **after** demineralizing:
58%   **8%**

See 'Tips and Recipe Ideas for: Multiple Beans' on page 75

GARBONZO BEANS
(Canned)

Approximate mineral concentration per 100 grams (about 3 ½ ounces) **before** demineralizing:

K 129 mg   P 74 mg

How to Mineral Reduce this Food

Step one: Empty the contents of a can into a sieve and rinse for 15 to 30 seconds under warm tap water (approximately 100°F) then allow them to drain briefly

Step two: Place beans in 4 times the volume (minimum of 1 quart per small can [about 1 cup] of beans) in warm tap water (approximately 100°F) stir vigorously for 15 – 20 seconds, and allow food to set for one hour on the counter.

Step three: After mineral reduction process has been completed, drain beans in a kitchen sieve.

Optimal Processing Time: 60 Minutes

Approximate mineral concentration per 100 grams (about 3 ½ ounces) **after** demineralizing:

K 32 mg   P 58 mg

Approximate mineral reduction potential **after** demineralizing:
75%   **22%**

See **'Tips and Recipe Ideas for: Multiple Beans'** on page 75

GREAT NORTHERN BEANS
(Canned)

Approximate mineral concentration per 100 grams (about 1/2 cup of drained beans) **before** demineralizing:

STOP

K 214 mg

GO

P 84 mg

How to Mineral Reduce this Food

Step one: Empty the contents of a can into a sieve and rinse for 15 to 30 seconds under warm tap water (approximately 100°F) then allow them to drain briefly.

Author's note – To achieve the maximum mineral reduction, each bean *should* be cut at least once (preferably across the largest segment). This can be done quickly by pouring the beans onto a flat surface, using a long-blade bread knife, press down on groups of beans cutting them (approximately) in half. Return the cut beans to the sieve and rinse with warm tap water once again.

Step two: Place beans in 4 times the volume (minimum of 1 quart per small can [about 1 cup] of beans) in warm tap water (approximately 100°F) stir vigorously for 15 – 20 seconds, and allow food to set for one hour on the counter

Step three: After mineral reduction process has been completed, drain beans in a kitchen sieve.

Optimal Processing Time: 60 Minutes

Approximate mineral concentration per 100 grams (about 3 ½ ounces) **after** demineralizing:

GO

K 38 mg

GO

P 51mg

Approximate mineral reduction potential **after** demineralizing:
82%   **39%**

See 'Tips and Recipe Ideas for: Multiple Beans' on page 75

KIDNEY BEANS
(Dry)

Approximate mineral concentration per 100 grams (about 2/3 cup of dry beans) **before** demineralizing:

STOP

K 215 mg

GO

P 104 mg

How to Mineral Reduce this Food

Step one: Measure out the desired amount of dried beans. Place in a sieve and rinse for 30 seconds under warm tap water (approximately 100°F). Checking for stones and other non-food material.

Step two: Place dried beans in 4 times the volume (1 quart minimum for 1 cup of beans) of **boiling water** and stir intermittently, dispersing the beans completely. Allow water to come to a rolling boil once again. Boil 10 - 15 minutes, remove container from the heat and allow it to set for one hour.

Step three: At the end of the time, pour beans into a kitchen sieve.

Author's note – To achieve the maximum mineral reduction, each bean *should* be cut at least once (preferably across the largest segment). This can be done quickly by pouring the beans onto a flat surface, using a long-blade bread knife, press down on groups of beans cutting them (approximately) in half. Return the cut beans to the sieve and rinse with warm tap water once again

Step four: Refill the container with fresh **warm** tap water, (approximately 100°F), same volume as before, and stir for 15 – 20 seconds. Now allow food to set on the counter for one hour, then drain.

Optimal Processing Time: 2 Hours **

Approximate mineral concentration per 100 grams (about 3 ½ ounces) **after** demineralizing:

GO

K <95 mg

GO

P <98 mg

Approximate mineral reduction potential **after** demineralizing:
<56%   <6%

See 'Tips and Recipe Ideas for: Multiple Beans' on page 75

Tips and Recipe Ideas for: Multiple Beans
(Black Beans, Butter Beans, Garbonzo Beans, Great Northern Beans, Kidney Beans)

** The degree of mineral reduction achieved depends on the permeability of the bean. If the beans are not going to be cut, this author suggests that the beans be subjected to an additional demineralization time of **four** hours, using the following instructions:

Step five: After Step four, refill once again with cold tap water (same volume) and replace in the refrigerator. Allow food to remain in the refrigerator until the end of the demineralization period.

There is no end to what you can do with a bean. Here are a few ideas to whet your appetite – and remember that ALL vegetables, and meats, mentioned here are demineralized before you add them to these recipes.

Bean Soup Bonanza
This soup can be as simple or as complicated as you want it to be.

Use 1/3 can equivalent of each of the following beans: Butter beans, Red beans, Kidney beans, Black Beans, Garbonzo beans, and Great Northern beans*.
*(Note - you can use as few or as many different beans as you wish, just be sure to adjust your recipe for 2 cups, final volume, or reduce the remainder of the ingredient accordingly);

Bring beans to a boil in as much water as you want to serve at the end;
Add ½ TSP of salt;
Boil, stirring regularly – mash beans slightly while cooking;
In a fry pan, slowly cook:
>   Margarine,
>   1 clove of minced garlic,
>   1 medium onion (minced)
>   ¾ cup of finely chopped sweet pepper
Add a little shaved ham or crumbled hamburger – let your taste buds decide how much;
Now cook the mix slowly together with a couple of glasses of water;
Season with a little vegetable spice mix, dash, or other no-salt seasoning;
Optional ingredients: parsley, bay leaf, grated pepper;
Add all of this to the bean blend and continue to slowly simmer until flavors 'meld'.

LIMA BEANS
(Canned)

Approximate mineral concentration per 100 grams (about ½ cup) **before** demineralizing:

STOP

K 306 mg

GO

P 70 mg

How to Mineral Reduce this Food

Step one: Empty the contents of a can into a sieve and rinse for 15 to 30 seconds under warm tap water (approximately 100°F) then allow them to drain briefly.

Step two: Place beans in 4 times the volume (minimum of 1 quart per small can [about 1 cup] of beans) in warm tap water (approximately 100°F) stir vigorously for 15 – 20 seconds, and allow food to set for one hour on the counter

Step three: After mineral reduction process has been completed, drain beans into a kitchen sieve

Optimal Processing Time: 60 Minutes

Approximate mineral concentration per 100 grams (about 3 ½ ounces or ½ cup) **after** demineralizing:

GO

K 84 mg

GO

P 51 mg

Approximate mineral reduction potential **after** demineralizing:
73%   27%

See 'Tips and Recipe Ideas for: Multiple Beans' on page 75

Recipe Ideas for: Lima Beans

Three Bean Salad
Numerous beans can be part of a bean salad. Here is a simple but tasty option – again, all vegetables and meats mentioned in this book are demineralized **before** using.

Use 1 cup of each bean or legume:
     Lima beans
     Green beans
     Yellow beans
Add 1 part vinegar to 2 parts water – sugar to taste. Chill and serve.
For best taste 'melding', refrigerate overnight.

Mixed vegetables
Add lima beans to a mixture of peas, green beans and/or carrots;
Cook till desired tenderness is reached. Top with no-trans-fatty acid margarine.

Beans and ham
Cook slivered ham with lima beans, and enough water to simmer;
Add bay leaf, Dash, or meat seasoning (optional);
Simmer very slowly until desired flavor is achieved.

PEANUTS
(Raw – Valencia peanuts)

Approximate mineral concentration per 100 grams (about 3 ½ ounces) **before** demineralizing:

K 573 mg   P 394 mg

How to Mineral Reduce this Food

Step one: Break or crush raw peanuts. This can be accomplished in one of several ways: (1) by placing the peanuts in a blender – on low speed – for one or two seconds; (2) by placing them in a plastic sack and hitting them lightly with a hammer (or a meat tenderizer), or, (3) placing them on a towel-covered hard surface and rolling over them lightly with a rolling pin.

Step two: Place peanuts in about 4 times the volume (minimum of 1 quart per 1 cup of broken peanuts) of boiling water. Boil for 5 full minutes, remove from heat, stir vigorously for 15 – 20 seconds, and allowed peanuts to set for one hour on the counter.

Step three: After mineral reduction process has been completed, drain peanuts by pouring into a small meshed kitchen sieve. After peanuts have been thoroughly drained, place peanuts on a cookie sheet and dry in an oven on low heat (approximately 250°F). When dry, store in the refrigerator or freezer.

Optimal Processing Time: approximately 65 Minutes

Approximate mineral concentration per 100 grams (about 3 ½ ounces) **after** demineralizing:

K 301 mg   P 260 mg

Approximate mineral reduction potential **after** demineralizing:
47%   **34%**

Tips and Recipe Ideas for: Peanuts

Peanuts - *to your health*

Peanuts have been enjoyed as a tasty snack for many years before their potential health benefits were known. Today peanuts are recognized as a good source of monounsaturated fats, vitamin E, niacin, folate, and minerals. They also contain resveratrol, a phenolic substance found in red grapes and red wine, and one which is receiving attention in medical literature. Some scientific studies have suggested a link between peanut consumption and: (1) a reduction in the risk of cardiovascular disease, (2) a possible aid in preventing gallstones, and (3) a potential positive association in the prevention of Alzheimer's and Age-related Cognitive Decline.

Peanuts, a few cautionary notes *

Allergens

While the peanut has enjoyed many favorable health reviews in recent years, it is wise to remember that this legume still has a dark side. Though any food can potentially induce an allergenic reaction, the peanut has proven more problematic then most. Research reveals an estimated one in every two hundred people may be allergic to the peanut (and other nuts as well), while as high as one in a hundred persons may already be sensitized without knowing it. The problem revolves around the proteins found in peanuts and how our immune system views these foreign intruders to our respiratory and digestive systems.

The Institute of Child Health Web site (**www.ich.ucl.ac.uk/factsheets/families/F000279/**) is a good source of information with regard to allergic response to peanuts.

*None of the demineralization procedures used in this book are expected to have any impact on the peanut protein-sensitive issue.

Oxalates

Peanuts are one of the few foods containing oxalate (rhubarb is another). People with severe chronic kidney disease or ESRD frequently have a higher than normal oxalate level because of their diminished renal capacity and inability to effectively void it. Oxalates are important because of their potential to cause numerous health problems. Persons with severe kidney or gallbladder problems are usually urged to avoid eating peanuts.

Goitrogens

Peanuts contain a substance that can interfere with the function of the thyroid gland. This can be an important issue if you have preexisting, untreated thyroid problems.

Read more about peanuts at the following Web addresses:
The Worlds Healthiest Foods - www.whfoods.com/genpage.php?tname=foodspice&dbid=101
The Peanut Institute - www.peanut-institute.org/HealthyDiets.html

RED BEANS
(Canned)

Approximate mineral concentration per 100 grams (about 3 ½ ounces) **before** demineralizing:

K 164 mg   P 82 mg

How to Mineral Reduce this Food

Step one: Empty the contents of a can into a sieve and rinse for 15 to 30 seconds under warm tap water (approximately 100°F) then allow them to drain briefly.

Step two: Place beans in 4 times the volume (minimum of 1 quart per small can [about 1 cup] of beans) in warm tap water (approximately 100°F) stir vigorously for 15 – 20 seconds, and allow food to set for one hour on the counter

Step three: After mineral reduction process has been completed, drain beans into a kitchen sieve.

Optimal Processing Time: 60 Minutes

Approximate mineral concentration per 100 grams (about 3 ½ ounces) **after** demineralizing:

K 48 mg   P 60 mg

Approximate mineral reduction potential **after** demineralizing:
>71%   >27%

See 'Tips and Recipe Ideas for: Multiple Beans' on page 75

PINTO BEANS
(Canned)

Approximate mineral concentration per 100 grams (about 3 ½ ounces) **before** demineralizing:

(GO)   (GO)

K 97 mg   **P** 75 mg

How to Mineral Reduce this Food

Authors note – The pinto beans tested by this author had a very low initial phosphorus and potassium load – lower than any other bean tested for this book.

Step one: Empty the contents of a can into a sieve and rinse for 15 to 30 seconds under warm tap water (approximately 100°F) then allow them to drain briefly. This step also aids in removing much of the salt added by the manufacturer.

Step two: Place beans in 4 times the volume (minimum of 1 quart per small can [about 1 cup] of beans) in warm tap water (approximately 100°F) stir vigorously for 15 – 20 seconds, and allow food to set for one hour on the counter

Step three: After mineral reduction process has been completed, drain beans into a kitchen sieve.

Optimal Processing Time: 60 Minutes

Approximate mineral concentration per 100 grams (about 3 ½ ounces) **after** demineralizing:

(GO)   (GO)

K 59 mg   **P** 52 mg

Approximate mineral reduction potential **after** demineralizing:
39%   **31%**

See 'Tips and Recipe Ideas for: Multiple Beans' on page 75

SOYBEANS
(Canned)

Approximate mineral concentration per 100 grams (about 1/2 - to 1/3 cup or 3 ½ ounces) **before** demineralizing:

<table>
<tr><td>⚠ CAUTION
K <170 mg</td><td>⚠ CAUTION
P <168 mg</td></tr>
</table>

Author's note – Potassium and phosphorus data for the 'control sample' of canned soybeans varied)

How to Mineral Reduce this Food

Step one: Empty the contents of a can into a sieve and rinse for 15 to 30 seconds under warm tap water (approximately 100°F) then allow them to drain briefly. This step also aids in removing much of the salt added by the manufacturer.

Author's note – To achieve the maximum mineral reduction, each bean *should* be cut at least once (preferably across the largest segment). This can be done quickly by pouring the beans onto a flat surface, using a long-blade bread knife, press down on groups of beans cutting them (approximately) in half. Return the cut beans to the sieve and rinse with warm tap water once again

Step two: Place beans in 4 times the volume (minimum of 1 quart per small can [about 1 cup] of beans) in warm tap water (approximately 100°F) stir vigorously for 15 – 20 seconds, and allow food to set for one hour on the counter

Step three: After mineral reduction process has been completed, drain beans into a kitchen sieve.

Optimal Processing Time: 60 Minutes

Approximate mineral concentration per 100 grams (about 3 ½ ounces) **after** demineralizing:

<table>
<tr><td>⚠ CAUTION
K 125 mg</td><td>⚠ CAUTION
P 145 mg</td></tr>
</table>

Approximate mineral reduction potential **after** demineralizing:
>26%   **>14%**

SOYBEANS
(Dried)

Approximate mineral concentration per 100 grams (about 1/2 to 1/3 cup or 3 ½ ounces) **before** demineralizing:

$$\text{STOP}$$

K 1010 mg

$$\text{STOP}$$

P 360 mg

How to Mineral Reduce this Food

Author's note – In order to achieve the maximum demineralization, in the most efficient manner, soybeans must be cracked or fragmented *before* beginning the process. A few bursts in a sturdy blender, or placing them in a plastic sack and hitting them with a hammer (or a meat tenderizer), should cause sufficient fragmentation.

Alternately, soybeans can be fragmented after **Step two,** however demineralization will not be as effective.

Step one: Measure out the desired amount of dried fragmented soybeans. Place in a sieve and rinse for 30 seconds under warm tap water (approximately 100°F). Checking for stones and other non-food material.

Step two: Place dried beans in 4 – 6 times the volume (1 ½ quart minimum for 1 cup of beans) of boiling water (add a tablespoon of oil to reduce foaming) and stir intermittently, dispersing the beans completely. Allow water to come to a rolling boil once again. Boil 15 - 20 minutes, remove container from the heat and allow it to stand for one hour.

Step three: At the end of the 1 hour you will notice that the water has darkened with the cooking residue of the soybeans. Pour beans into a kitchen sieve and rinse.

Step four: Refill the container with fresh water, same volume as before, bring to a boil and stir in soybeans.

Author's note – The following processing /cooking time and method is only one of several methods that can be used to mineral reduce this food.

Simmer soybeans for *at least* 15 – 45 minutes, depending upon how tender you wish the final product to be. Remove the container from the heat, and allow the contents to set one hour, then drain.

Step five: Replace water with cold tap water (same volume), place container in a refrigerator and allow beans to demineralize until the end of the recommended demineralization time period which is six hours.

Tips for Soybeans (canned and dried):

Note -- This author has seen cooking times ranging between a slow simmer on the stove for 30 to 60 minutes, to a 15 pound, 20 minute pressure cooking schedule. Follow the manufacturers' recommended pressure cooking time for your appliance. Once completed, allow food to set on the counter for one hour, then drain.

Optimal Processing Time: *variable* (8 hours is recommended)

Approximate mineral concentration per 100 grams (about 3 ½ ounces) **after** demineralizing:

After **Step four:** Potassium should be <120 mg
Phosphorus should be <190 mg

After **Step five:** Potassium should be   <35 mg
Phosphorus should be <150 mg

Numerous soybean recipes are available in various cookbooks and on the Web.

Did you Know -- Soybean fun facts

Because they contain all the essential amino acids, soybeans are considered a source of complete protein.

Soybeans are grown throughout the world – everywhere cultivation is possible.

Soybeans are extremely versatile – they may be eaten along with their pod, alone, or as one of many soy-relate preparation, such a Tofu, miso, natto, soy meal and flour products, oil, etc..

Soy has been made into a dairy and/or meat substitute, as well as products for industrial use.

Soy allergies are one of the more common food allergies.

SOY GRITS
(Dried - processed - soybean granules)

Approximate mineral concentration per 100 grams (about ½ cup or 3 ½ ounces of dry grits) **before** demineralizing:

STOP   STOP

K 2488 mg   P 514 mg

How to Mineral Reduce this Food

Note – The Soy Grits referred to in this book were purchased from <u>Fearn Natural Foods</u>, and are sold under the bran name *Soya granules.*

Step one: Measure out the desired amount of soy grits directly from the can

Step two: Place soy grits in 4 times the volume (1 quart minimum for 1 cup of grits) of boiling water (with a tablespoon of cooking oil to control foaming) and stir intermittently, dispersing the granules completely. Allow water to come to a rolling boil once again. Boil 10 - 15 minutes, remove container from the heat and allow it to set for one hour. It is OK (but not necessary) to stir the grits intermittently while they are setting.

Step three: At the end of this period, soy grits have swollen sufficiently so that they will be caught in a fine mesh kitchen sieve upon draining Drain water away by pouring the contents into a kitchen sieve. Refill the container with fresh cold tap water, same volume as before, stir grits vigorously for 15 to 20 seconds, and allowed food to set in the refrigerator for one hour then drain again.
While soy grits are draining, place several paper towels on top and press out as much moisture as possible. Alternately, the Soy Grits can be sandwiched between layers of paper toweling, placed on a working surface, and pressed. Be sure to store any uneaten demineralized soy grits in the freezer for later use

Optimal Processing Time: 2 Hours

Approximate mineral concentration per 100 grams (about 3 ½ ounces) **after** demineralizing:

CAUTION   CAUTION

K 117 mg   P 139 mg

Approximate mineral reduction potential **after** demineralizing:

95%   **74%**

Tips for: Soy grits

Soy grits are simply soybeans that have been pre-cooked, ground, and dried. The manufacturer recommends they be used in cold cereal, meat dishes, and vegetable dishes. Treat soy grits the same way you would any soy meal additive, by adding it directly to the vegetable or meat dish as you are cooking it. Demineralized soy grits have no real distinct flavor of their own, so for a well-round dish, be sure to simmer soy grits with food, allowing it to take up the 'identity' of the food it is being cooked with.

TOFU
(soft)

Approximate mineral concentration per 100 grams (about 3 ½ ounces) **before** demineralizing:

K 128 mg   P 124 mg

Note – This author has found that **hard** tofu demineralizes poorly. There is no data on 'medium' tofu.

How to Mineral Reduce this Food

Step one: Soft tofu is <u>very</u> fragile. Remove the soft tofu block from its carton. Place in a large plastic tray (capable of holding four such blocks) and cut into approximately ½ inch thick slabs. Now rinse carefully by slowly filling with cold tap water then draining. Repeat several times until the water is clear.

Step two: Refill container with cold water and place in refrigerator overnight. During the 24 hour cycle, change the water at least once (preferably twice).

Step three: After the twenty-four hour cycle is complete, be sure to change the tofu once again (cold water). Remember to always keep tofu submerged in cold water, and in the refrigerator. Follow manufacturers recommended storage time for this product.

Optimal Processing Time: Overnight

Approximate mineral concentration per 100 grams (about 3 ½ ounces) **after** demineralizing:

GO   CAUTION

K 44 mg   P 114 mg

Approximate mineral reduction potential **after** demineralizing:
66%   **8%**

MEATS

Meats – Take Note

All meats, as well as poultry and fish are naturally high in phosphorus and potassium. Manufacturers complicate matters by adding salt to processed selections, raising the sodium content. Take a look at the raw Vs. processes selections listed in this book – selections which are without additives have very low sodium content (i.e. **natural** raw beef hamburger compared to bologna, a processed product).

The use of food additives such as sodium phosphate or disodium phosphate, in raw meats adds entirely new dimensions to the problem. These additives can raise the total phosphate and sodium levels, of the meat you are preparing to eat, dramatically. Demineralization can reduce the added potassium, phosphate and sodium levels significantly. However, in meat that has been treated with sodium phosphate food additive, the total phosphorus content tends to remain higher then if the meat were not treated (i.e. *natural, organic, un-treated*).

Meats Tested

Bacon

Beef hamburger

Beef kidney

Beef liver

Beef strips

Bologna

Braunschweiger

Catfish

Chicken strips

Ham (canned and cured)

Hot dog

Mackerel

Ostrich (ground)

Pork (ground)

Salmon (canned and fresh)

Shrimp

Spam

Tuna

Turkey (ground)

Walleye

BACON
(Processed)

Approximate mineral concentration per 100 grams (about 3 ½ ounces) **before** demineralizing:

STOP   STOP   STOP

K 251 mg   P 216 mg   Na 753 mg

How to Mineral Reduce this Food

Step one: Place desired number bacon slices in a sieve and rinse for 10 to 15 seconds under warm tap water (approximately 100°F).

Step two: Place meat in warm water (approximately 100°F) – about one quart per 6 to 7 slices of bacon, for 30 minutes on the countertop. Stirring the bacon with your hand, or large spoon, helps distribute the meat.

Step three: After the 30 minutes, empty the bowl into a thoroughly clean sieve, rinse briefly, and squeeze in your hand. Place bacon between paper towels and press out excess water. Use immediately. If you plan to cook the meat another day, freeze demineralized bacon immediately. For food safety considerations, use non-frozen demineralized meat within 24 hours.

Optimal Processing Time: 30 Minutes

Approximate mineral concentration per 100 grams (about 3 ½ ounces) **after** demineralizing:

GO   GO   GO

K 11 mg   P 72 mg   Na 112 mg

Approximate mineral reduction potential **after** demineralizing:
96%   67%   85%

My tips for mineral reduced Bacon:

BEEF HAMBURGER
(Fresh - raw)

Approximate mineral concentration per 100 grams (about 3 ½ ounces) **before** demineralizing:

(STOP)	(CAUTION)	(GO)
K 216 mg	P 123 mg	Na 44 mg

*NOTE – If your beef has been injected with the food additive (sodium/disodium) phosphate, **see 'A Word About...Food Additives'**. The above values are for <u>non-injected</u> meats.

How to Mineral Reduce this Food

Step one: Open the package and discard the wrapper. Break ground meat apart in a sieve. Rinse all ground meats for 10 to 15 seconds under warm tap water (approximately 100°F) to remove the old tissue blood. Allow meat to drip out in a sieve before proceeding to step two

Step two: Place meat in warm water (approximately 100°F) for 30 minutes. Warm water demineralization is carried out in a thoroughly clean bowl, outside the refrigerator for 30 minutes (be sure to use a 2 quart minimum volume per pound of ground meat).

Step three: After the 30 minutes has been completed, empty the bowl into a thoroughly clean sieve, and rinse the meat for 10 to 15 seconds under cold running tap water. Ground meats will usually not pass through a kitchen sieve with small mesh to any significant extent

Place a paper towel on top of the meat and press out the excess water. Remove the meat from the sieve and place on a small stack of fresh, clean paper towels, on a clean working surface. Now gently press the remaining moisture out of the meat. Use immediately, or store the meat in a clean container, in the refrigerator, if you plan to cook the meat later the same day. If you plan to cook the meat another day, freeze demineralized meat immediately. For food safety considerations, use non-frozen demineralized meat within 24 hours.

Optimal Processing Time: 30 Minutes

Approximate mineral concentration per 100 grams (about 3 ½ ounces) **after** demineralizing:

(GO)	(GO)	(GO)
K 36 mg	P 70 mg	Na 9 mg

Approximate mineral reduction potential **after** demineralizing:
83%	43%	80%

Tips and Recipe Ideas: Beef Hamburger

Always handle food safely! This is **especially** important where meat is concerned. Review the section on **Food Safety**. If you have further questions, contact your renal dietitian or home-extension service.

Mineral-reduced meat will appear light colored because a great deal of the blood has also been removed during demineralization. This is normal.

Mineral-reduced meat should be cooked and eaten as soon as possible after processing, or refrigerated and used within 24 hours. Freeze any mineral-reduced meat that will not be used within 24 hours.

If you are planning to make burgers from your demineralized meat, be sure to remove excess moisture from demineralized meat before frying to avoid grease spattering. This can be done more effectively if, after draining in a sieve, ball the meat and place it on a couple of paper towels, then press firmly to remove most of the moisture. If you enjoy a zesty burger, try spicing things up with a bit of seasoning, or a dash of your favorite sauce.

Remember, hamburgers aren't the only use for mineral-reduced beef. Mineral-reduced meats can be used for any dish you would have made non-mineral-reduced. Why not try a mineral-reduced meatloaf, casserole.

Pizza time!

You can easily make a mineral reduced pizza. With the exception of the two wheat-flour tortilla shells you will use as the base, all the meats, vegetables, and cheeses are demineralized **before** use.

Double over a thick piece of aluminum foil, turning the edges up to catch any overflowed cheese. Alternately, a heavy aluminum pizza pan can be used.

Begin layering cheese (Swiss and/or cheddar cheese) between 2 tortilla shells - this will form the solid 'base' for the rest of the ingredients, once it has been melted.

On top of the top tortilla shell, spread a thin layer of either:

Ketchup **or** tomato paste with onion, garlic, a little sprinkle of sugar -- to taste, in the mix

Generous layer of cheese (any demineralized cheese)

Crumbled cooked hamburger

Minced black olives

Minced green and red peppers

Minced corn, and artichokes

Add another layer cheese
Bake at 350F – 375F until nice and bubbly and hot all the way through.
Eat and enjoy!

Meatloaf Magic
There are as many meatloaf recipes as there are chefs preparing them. Here is yet another one.

Remember, all meat and vegetable ingredients are demineralized in advance.

Slowly simmer the following ingredients in pan with no-trans-fat margarine:
      1 medium, red onion – finely chopped
      1 cup of green or red peppers
Now cool slightly and set aside.
In another pan, add ½ to 1 cup of soy grits, and a dash of:
      (The following spices are not demineralized)
      Onion powder
      Garlic powder
      Paprika
      Mrs. Dash
      A pinch of salt
Mix – taste – add a small amount of sugar to taste. Now add:
      4 slices of cubed French bread
      3 egg whites
      ¼ cup of ketchup
      A pinch of salt (optional)

Add the contents of the meat pan and stir thoroughly (1/2 lb of processed hamburger).

Pack into a microwave pan and cover during the first 5 minutes of cooking – open – drain excess juice – put BBQ sauce as desired on top – finish microwaving – cover and let stand 15 more minutes.

Serve and enjoy!

Remember to store any uneaten meatloaf in the refrigerator – it is great cold as well!

My Tips for mineral reduced Meatloaf:

_____

_____

_____

_____

_____

_____

_____

_____

_____

_____

_____

_____

_____

_____

_____

_____

_____

_____

_____

_____

_____

_____

_____

_____

BEEF KIDNEY
(Fresh)

Approximate mineral concentration per 100 grams (about 3 ½ ounces) **before** demineralizing:

K 227 mg   P 233 mg

How to Mineral Reduce this Food

Author's note – In order to demineralize effectively, beef kidney must be cut into strips no thicker than ¼ inch. This is best accomplished when the kidney is slightly frosty. If you are concerned about cholesterol, you may wish to open the kidney and clean out the visible fat before proceeding.

Step one: Cut the kidney into strips of approximately ¼ inch in thickness or less. Rinse kidney under warm tap water (approximately 100°F), squeezing it in your hand until the majority of the visible blood has been washed away. Drain briefly in a sieve.

Step two: Place beef kidney strips in warm water (approximately 100°F) - 2 quarts for one pound or 3 quarts for two pounds (minimum volume) for 30 minutes. Stir vigorously to disperse the strips. Warm water demineralization is carried out in a thoroughly clean bowl, outside of the refrigerator. At the end of 30 minutes, drain into a kitchen colander or sieve.

Step three: Return kidney strips to the demineralization bowl and add cold tap water (same volume as before) then place it in the refrigerator for two hours. For the best results, change the water after the first hour, refilling with cold tap water. At the end of the demineralization time, drain meat in a sieve, and remove excess moisture by placing it on a small stack of paper towels.

Optimal Processing Time: 2 Hours and 30 Minutes **

Approximate mineral concentration per 100 grams (about 3 ½ ounces) **after** demineralizing:

K 43 mg   P 142 mg

Approximate mineral reduction potential **after** demineralizing:
81%   **39%**

Tips for: Beef Kidney

** Beef kidney can be left in cold water (in the refrigerator) overnight without sacrificing taste. If you plan to carry out overnight demineralization, be sure to change the water once again before retiring to bed. Further mineral reduction will naturally occur.

My Tips for mineral reduced Beef Kidney:

_____
_____
_____
_____
_____
_____
_____
_____
_____
_____
_____
_____
_____
_____
_____
_____
_____
_____
_____
_____
_____

BEEF LIVER
(Fresh)

Approximate mineral concentration per 100 grams (about 3 ½ ounces) **before** demineralizing:

K 249 mg   P 284 mg

How to Mineral Reduce this Food

Author's note – In order to demineralize effectively, all solid chunks of meat must be cut into ¼ inch thick strips. This applies to liver as well, and is easily done when liver is slightly frosty.

Step one: Cut liver into strips of approximately ¼ inch in thickness or less. Rinse under warm tap water (approximately 100°F), squeezing it in your hand until the majority of the visible blood has been washed away. Drain briefly in a sieve.

Step two: Place liver strips in warm water (approximately 100°F) - 2 quart for one pound or 3 quarts for two pounds (minimum volume) for 30 minutes. Stir vigorously to disperse the strips. Warm water demineralization is carried out in a thoroughly clean bowl, outside of the refrigerator. At the end of 30 minutes, drain in a kitchen colander or sieve.

Step three: Return liver strips to the demineralization bowl and add cold tap water (same volume as before) then place it in the refrigerator for three hours. For the best results, change the water after the first hour, refilling with cold tap water. At the end of the demineralization time, drain liver in a sieve, and remove excess moisture by placing it on a small stack of paper towels.

Optimal Processing Time: 3 Hours and 30 Minutes*
(Potential Mineral Reduction after 8 Hours and 30 Minutes) **

Approximate mineral concentration per 100 grams (about 3 ½ ounces) **after** demineralizing:

     * K 74 mg   *P 143 mg
     **K 19 mg   **P 125 mg

Approximate mineral reduction potential **after** demineralizing:
     *70%   *50%
     ** 92%   **56%

Tips for: Beef Liver

Beef liver can be demineralized further by leaving it in cold water (in the refrigerator) overnight without sacrificing taste. If you plan to carry out overnight demineralization, be sure to change the water once again before retiring to bed. Further mineral reduction will naturally occur.

My Tips for mineral reduced Beef Liver:

_____

_____

_____

_____

_____

_____

_____

_____

_____

_____

_____

_____

_____

_____

_____

_____

_____

_____

_____

BEEF STRIPS
(Fresh)

Approximate mineral concentration per 100 grams (about 3 ½ ounces) **before** demineralizing:

K 232 mg   **P** 131 mg

*NOTE – If your beef has been injected with the food additive (sodium/disodium) phosphate, see: **'A Word About....Food Additives'**. The above values are for <u>non-injected</u> meats.

How to Mineral Reduce this Food

Author's Note -- In order to demineralize effectively, all solid chunks of meat must be cut into ¼ inch thick strips. This is easily done when meat is slightly frosty.

Step one: Cut beef into strips of approximately ¼ inch in thickness or less. Rinse under **warm** tap water (approximately 100ºF), squeezing it in your hand until the majority of the visible blood has been washed away. Drain briefly in a sieve.

Step two: Place beef strips in warm water (approximately 100ºF) - 2 quart for one pound or 3 quarts for two pounds (minimum volume) for 30 minutes. Stir vigorously to disperse the strips. Warm water demineralization is carried out in a thoroughly clean bowl outside of the refrigerator. At the end of 30 minutes, drain into a kitchen colander or sieve, then squeeze out as much liquid as possible.

Step three: Place strips in cold tap water (same volume as before) in the refrigerator for one hour. At the end of the demineralization time, drain, then remove excess moisture by placing it on a small stack of paper towels.

Optimal Processing Time: 1 Hour and 30 Minutes*****
(Potential Mineral Reduction after 8 Hours and 30 Minutes) ******

Optimal Processing Time: 90 Minutes
Approximate mineral concentration per 100 grams (about 3 ½ ounces) **after** demineralizing:

GO   GO

*K 19 mg   ***P** 67 mg
K 4 mg   ****P 61 mg
Approximate mineral reduction potential **after** demineralizing:
*92%   ***49%**
98%   ****53%

Tips for: Beef Strips

Beef strips can be demineralized further by leaving it in cold water (in the refrigerator) overnight without sacrificing taste. If you plan to carry out overnight demineralization, be sure to change the water once again before retiring to bed. Further mineral reduction will naturally occur.

My Tips for mineral reduced Beef Strips:

_____

_____

_____

_____

_____

_____

_____

_____

_____

_____

_____

_____

_____

_____

_____

_____

_____

_____

_____

BOLOGNA
(Processed cold meat – sliced into 1/8 inch slices by company)

Approximate mineral concentration per 100 grams (about 3 ½ ounces) **before** demineralizing:

STOP	CAUTION	STOP
K 227 mg	P 145 mg	Na 962 mg

How to Mineral Reduce this Food

Step one: Remove desired number of bologna slices and rinse thoroughly under warm tap water (approximately 100°F) rubbing each slice briskly (but gently) with your hand.

Step two: Place bologna slices in warm water (approximately 100°F). Use a minimum of one quart for 5 slices. Allow processed meat to set on the counter for 30 minutes.

Step three: At the end of the demineralization time, drain the water, then place on a small stack of paper towels and press gently.

Optimal Processing Time: 30 Minutes

Approximate mineral concentration per 100 grams (about 3 ½ ounces) **after** demineralizing:

GO	GO	GO
K 19 mg	P 72 mg	Na 111 mg

Approximate mineral reduction potential **after** demineralizing:

92%	50%	88%

My Tips for mineral reduced Bologna:

_____

_____

_____

_____

_____

_____

_____

_____

_____

_____

_____

_____

_____

_____

_____

_____

_____

_____

_____

_____

_____

_____

_____

_____

BRAUNSCHWEIGER
(Process cold meat – sliced into 1/8 inch slices by company)

Approximate mineral concentration per 100 grams (about 3 ½ ounces) **before** demineralizing:

STOP   STOP   STOP

K 671 mg   P 209 mg   Na 954 mg

How to Mineral Reduce this Food

Author's note – Braunschweiger is an especially fatty meat. Because of this, demineralization is less efficient. Nevertheless, a 30 minute demineralization process will have an impact on the final mineral value.
If your Braunschweiger has not been pre cut it is important that you cut it as thinly as possible. This can best be accomplished by cutting it with a <u>very sharp</u> knife when it is slightly frozen.

Step one: Remove the outer packaging, but <u>do not</u> remover the inner plastic wrapping around the meat. Braunschweiger crumbles very easily when demineralized without an exterior support. If, however, crumbling does not concern you, go ahead and remove the ring.
Reducing this processed meat to large crumbles will aid in demineralization. Place directly into **warm** tap water (approximately 100°F) one quart minimum per ¼ lb. You will notice a grease layer forming in a few minutes. It is OK to slowly drain away this water and refill with warm tap water once again, just be careful not to let the Braunschweiger slip from the bowl.

Step two: Allow processing meat to set on the counter for 30 minutes. At the end of the demineralization time, drain water away carefully then slide the Braunschweiger onto a small stack of paper towels and pat gently to remove excess moisture.

Optimal Processing Time: 30 Minutes

Approximate mineral concentration per 100 grams (about 3 ½ ounces) **after** demineralizing:

CAUTION   CAUTION   STOP

K 188 mg   P 158 mg   Na 458 mg

Approximate mineral reduction potential **after** demineralizing:
72%   24%   52%

My Tips for mineral reduced Braunschweiger:

CATFISH
(Fresh or frozen – fillets)

Approximate mineral concentration per 100 grams (about 3 ½ ounces) **before** demineralizing:

K 254 mg   P 176 mg

How to Mineral Reduce this Food

Author's note – In order to demineralize effectively, catfish fillets must be cut into ¼ inch thick strips. This is easily done when meat is slightly frosty – not frozen solid.

Step one: Cut into strips of approximately ¼ inch in thickness or less. Rinse under warm tap water (approximately 100°F), squeezing it in your hand *very gently*

Step two: Place fish in warm water (approximately 100°F) - 1 quart for one pound (minimum volume) for 30 minutes. Stir gently to disperse. Warm water demineralization is carried out in a thoroughly clean bowl outside of the refrigerator. At the end of 30 minutes, drain into a kitchen colander or sieve. Carefully squeeze out as much liquid as possible.

Step three: Place strips in cold tap water (same volume as before) in the refrigerator for 4 hour. At the end of the demineralization time, drain, then remove excess moisture by placing between a small stack of paper towels and pressing gently.

Optimal Processing Time: 4 Hours and 30 Minutes

Approximate mineral concentration per 100 grams (about 3 ½ ounces) **after** demineralizing:

(GO)   (GO)

K 75 mg   P 71 mg

Approximate mineral reduction potential **after** demineralizing:
70%   **60%**

My Tips for mineral reduced Catfish:

CHICKEN STRIPS
(Fresh-raw)

Approximate mineral concentration per 100 grams (about 3 ½ ounces) **before** demineralizing:

(STOP)	(STOP)	(GO)
K 287 mg	P 201 mg	Na 67 mg

*****NOTE** – If your chicken has been injected with the food additive (sodium/disodium) phosphate, **see** 'A Word About...Food Additives'. The above values are for <u>non-injected</u> meats.

How to Mineral Reduce this Food

Step one: Open the package and discard the wrapper. Raw chicken cuts best when slightly frosty. Be sure to remove all skin and visible fat before cutting strips of meat. For best demineralization results, strips should be no thicker than ¼" in thickness. Measure out the desired amount of meat, place into a thoroughly clean sieve and rinse vigorously under warm tap water (approximately 100°F) for 1 minute.

Step two: Place one pound of chicken strips in a minimum of 2 quarts of cold tap water (or 2 – 4 pounds of chicken strips in 3 quarts). Stir for 15 – 20 seconds and allowed food to setand for one hour in the refrigerator. Chicken strips can be demineralized for an additional hour without loss of taste, however, additional mineral removal will be minimal. To continue the process, simply replace the water after the end of the first hour, with fresh cold tap water, and return it to the refrigerator until the end of the second hour.

Step three: At the end of the mineral-reduction time, drain meat in a sieve, then remove excess moisture by placing it on a small stack of paper towels. Blot dry if necessary.

Optimal Processing Time: 60 Minutes

Approximate mineral concentration per 100 grams (about 3 ½ ounces) **after** demineralizing:

Sliced:	(GO)	(GO)	---
Thin (about ¼")	K 68 mg	P 96 mg	Na *not done*
Thick (about ½")	K 208 mg	P 176 mg	Na 28 mg
	(STOP)	CAUTION	(GO)

Approximate mineral reduction potential **after** demineralizing:

Thin	64%	48%	*not done*
Thick	28%	12%	58%

Tips for: Chicken Strips

Always handle food safely! This is **especially** important where meat is concerned. Review the section on **Food Safety**. If you have further questions, contact your renal dietitian or home-extension service.

Mineral-reduced meat will appear light colored because a great deal of the blood has also been removed during demineralization. This is normal.

Mineral-reduced meat should be cooked and eaten as soon as possible after processing, or refrigerated and used within 24 hours. Freeze any mineral-reduced meat that will not be used within 24 hours. Remove as much of the moisture before frying to avoid grease 'spattering'. After draining in a sieve, place it on a couple of paper towels then press firmly to remove most of the moisture. Once the water has been removed, cook as desired, or store in the refrigerator overnight.

HAM
(Canned)

Approximate mineral concentration per 100 grams (about 3 ½ ounces) **before** demineralizing:

STOP	STOP	STOP
K 292 mg	**P** 250 mg	**Na** 1104 mg

How to Mineral Reduce this Food

Step one: Unless ham has been pre-sliced, slice ham into ¼" thickness. Now rinse vigorously under warm tap water (approximately 100°F) for 1 minute and let drain.

Step two: Place ham in a minimum of 4 times the volume of boiling water (about 2 quarts per ½ pound of ham, 3 quarts per pound) and stir continuously. Boil for 5 minutes.

Author's note – Canned ham has been processed with materials to bind the meat, salt, and spices into a stable shape and thus require longer boiling times to reduce the mineral load.

Step three: Empty into a sieve and rinse with cold tap water to cool the meat. Place on several paper towels to remove the maximum amount of moisture.

Optimal Processing Time: Approximately 5 Minutes

Approximate mineral concentration per 100 grams (about 3 ½ ounces) **after** demineralizing:

GO	CAUTION	CAUTION
K 55 mg	**P** 121 mg	**Na** 221 mg

Approximate mineral reduction potential **after** demineralizing:
81%	**52%**	**80%**

My Tips for mineral reduced canned Ham:

HAM
(Cured)

Approximate mineral concentration per 100 grams (about 3 ½ ounces) **before** demineralizing:

(GO)   ⚠ CAUTION   [STOP]

K 64 mg   P 121 mg   Na 260 mg

How to Mineral Reduce this Food

Step one: Unless ham has been pre-sliced, slice ham into ¼" thickness. Now rinse vigorously under warm tap water (approximately 100°F) for 1 minute and let drain.

Step two: Place ham in a minimum of 4 times the volume of boiling water (about 2 quarts per ½ pound of ham, 3 quarts per pound) and stir continuously. Boil for only 1 or 2 minutes.

Author's note –Regular "cured" ham has only been *injected* with salt/spices/etc., and hence requires very little boiling time to effectively demineralize it. *Canned* ham has been processed with materials to bind the meat, salt, and spices into a stable shape and thus require longer boiling times to reduce the mineral load.

Step three: Quickly pour into a sieve and rinse with cold tap water to cool the meat. Place on several paper towels to remove the maximum amount of moisture.

Optimal Processing Time: 1 - 2 Minutes

Approximate mineral concentration per 100 grams (about 3 ½ ounces) **after** demineralizing:

(GO)   ⚠ CAUTION   (GO)

K 45 mg   P 117 mg   Na 107 mg

Approximate mineral reduction potential **after** demineralizing:
30%   **3%**   **59%**

My Tips for mineral reduced cured Ham:

HOT DOGS
(Processed meat)

Approximate mineral concentration per 100 grams (about 3 ½ ounces) **before** demineralizing:

CAUTION   STOP   STOP

K 155 mg   P 222 mg   Na 1379 mg

How to Mineral Reduce this Food

Note -- Hot dogs tend to float more readily when they are cut crosswise. This author recommends that hot dogs be sliced *lengthwise* to greatly reduce the tendency to float during processing.

Step one: Slice hot dogs lengthwise into ¼" thickness. Now rinse vigorously under warm tap water (approximately 100°F) for 1 minute and let drain.

Step two: Place hot dogs in a minimum of 4 times the volume of boiling water (about 2 quarts per ½ pound of cut hot dogs, 3 quarts per pound) and stir continuously. Boil for at least 7 minutes.

Author's note -- Hot dogs have been processed with materials to bind meat, salt, and spices into a stable shape and thus require longer boiling times to effectively penetrate the binding materials and demineralize them.

Step three: Quickly pour into a sieve and rinse with cold tap water to cool the meat. Place on several paper towels to remove the maximum amount of moisture.

Optimal Processing Time: 7 Minutes

Approximate mineral concentration per 100 grams (about 3 ½ ounces) **after** demineralizing:

GO   CAUTION   STOP

K 77 mg   P 172 mg   Na 551 mg

Approximate mineral reduction potential **after** demineralizing:
50%   **23%**   **60%**

My Tips for mineral reduced Hot Dogs:

MACKEREL
(Canned)

Approximate mineral concentration per 100 grams (about 3 ½ ounces) **before** demineralizing:

STOP	STOP	STOP
K 229 mg	P 334 mg	Na 334 mg

How to Mineral Reduce this Food

Step one: Open the can, empty contents into a sieve and break into small chunks. Rinse under **warm** tap water (approximately 100°F) for 15 to 20 seconds.

Step two: Place mackerel in warm water (approximately 100°F) for 30 minutes. Warm water demineralization is carried out in a thoroughly clean bowl outside the refrigerator. Use about 1 - 2 quarts of water per 1 or 2, 6-oz cans of mackerel.

Step three: Quickly pour into a sieve and rinse with cold tap water to cool the fish. Place on several paper towels to remove the maximum amount of moisture.

Optimal Processing Time: 30 Minutes

Approximate mineral concentration per 100 grams (about 3 ½ ounces) **after** demineralizing:

GO	STOP	CAUTION
K 60 mg	P 238 mg	Na 208 mg

Approximate mineral reduction potential **after** demineralizing:
| 74% | 29% | 38% |

My Tips for mineral reduced Mackerel:

OSTRICH
(Fresh - ground)

Approximate mineral concentration per 100 grams (about 3 ½ ounces) **before** demineralizing:

K 110 mg   P 191 mg

How to Mineral Reduce this Food

Step one: Break ground ostrich meat apart in a sieve. Rinse for 10 to 15 seconds under warm tap water (approximately 100°F) to remove the old tissue blood. Allow meat to drip out in a sieve before proceeding to step two

Step two: Place meat in warm water (approximately 100°F) for 30 minutes. Warm water demineralization is carried out in a thoroughly clean bowl, outside of the refrigerator. Be sure to use a 2 quart minimum volume per pound of ground ostrich.

Step three: Empty the bowl into a thoroughly clean sieve, and rinse the meat for 10 to 15 seconds under cold running tap water to cool. Ground meats will usually not pass through a kitchen colander or sieve with small holes, to any significant extent Place a paper towel on top of the meat and press out the excess water. Remove the meat from the sieve and place on a small stack of fresh paper towels, on a clean working surface. Now gently press the remaining moisture out of the meat. Use immediately, or store the meat in a clean container, in the refrigerator, if you plan to cook the meat later the same day. If you plan to cook the meat another day, freeze demineralized meat immediately. For food safety considerations, use non-frozen demineralized meat within 24 hours.

Optimal Processing Time: 30 Minutes

Approximate mineral concentration per 100 grams (about 3 ½ ounces) **after** demineralizing:

GO   GO

K 36 mg   P 63 mg

Approximate mineral reduction potential **after** demineralizing:
67%   **>67%**

Tips for Ostrich:

Ostrich meat has been available and served in the United States since 1992. This meat has a fine red texture with a flavor similar to beef. Ostrich is naturally lower in fat content by two-thirds. Because of its low fat content, ostrich tends to cook faster than other meats. In general, the American Ostrich Association says that cooking methods used for veal works well with ostrich. Cooking ostrich to well done is not recommended.

My Tips for mineral reduced Ostrich:

_____

_____

_____

_____

_____

_____

_____

_____

_____

_____

_____

_____

_____

_____

_____

_____

PORK
(Fresh – ground)

Approximate mineral concentration per 100 grams (about 3 ½ ounces) **before** demineralizing:

K 172 mg   P 196 mg

*NOTE – If your pork has been injected with the food additive (sodium/disodium) phosphate, **see 'A Word About...Food Additives'**. The above values are for non-injected meats.

How to Mineral Reduce this Food

Step one: Break ground pork apart into a sieve. Rinse for 10 to 15 seconds under warm tap water (approximately 100°F) to remove the old tissue blood. Allow meat to drip out in a sieve before proceeding to step two.

Step two: Place meat in warm water (approximately 100°F) for 30 minutes. Warm water demineralization is carried out in a thoroughly clean bowl outside of the refrigerator. Be sure to use a 2 quart minimum volume per pound of ground pork.

Step three: Empty the bowl into a thoroughly clean sieve, and rinse the meat for 10 to 15 seconds under cold running tap water to cool ground meats. The meat will usually not pass through a kitchen sieve with small holes, to any significant extent. Place a paper towel on top of the meat and press out the excess water. Remove the meat from the sieve and place on a small stack of clean paper towels, on a clean working surface. Now gently press the remaining moisture out of the meat. Use immediately, or store the meat in a clean container, in the refrigerator, if you plan to cook the meat later the same day. If you plan to cook the meat another day, freeze demineralized meat immediately. For food safety considerations, use non-frozen demineralized meat within 24 hours.

Optimal Processing Time: 30 Minutes

Approximate mineral concentration per 100 grams (about 3 ½ ounces) **after** demineralizing:

K 57 mg   P 80 mg

Approximate mineral reduction potential **after** demineralizing:
67%   59%

My Tips for mineral reduced ground Pork:

_____

_____

_____

_____

_____

_____

_____

_____

_____

_____

_____

_____

_____

_____

_____

_____

_____

_____

_____

_____

_____

_____

_____

_____

SALMON
(Canned)

Approximate mineral concentration per 100 grams (about 3 ½ ounces) **before** demineralizing:

STOP	STOP	GO
K 277 mg	P 229 mg	Na 136 mg

How to Mineral Reduce this Food

Step one: Open the can, empty contents into a sieve and break salmon into small chunks. Rinse under warm tap water (approximately 100°F) for 15 to 20 seconds.

Step two: Place salmon in warm water (approximately 100°F) for 30 minutes. Warm water demineralization is carried out in a thoroughly clean bowl outside the refrigerator. Use about 1 - 2 quarts of water per 1 large can of salmon.

Step three: Quickly pour the contents of the bowl into a sieve and rinse with cold tap water to cool the fish. Place salmon on several paper towels to remove the maximum amount of moisture.

Optimal Processing Time: 30 Minutes

Approximate mineral concentration per 100 grams (about 3 ½ ounces) **after** demineralizing:

GO	CAUTION	GO
K 46 mg	P 159 mg	Na 64 mg

Approximate mineral reduction potential **after** demineralizing:

80%	31%	53%

Author's note - Mineral reduced canned salmon is very mild.

Recipe Ideas for canned Salmon:

Salmon Burgers

Here is an easy alternative to beef burgers.

To one can of demineralized salmon, add:
> Crumbs of 5 –7 no-salt soda crackers
> A whole egg
> Spices (sage, poultry seasoning, or Dash) to taste

Mix thoroughly, form into patties, and place in a well-oiled pan, or use no-trans-fat margarine;
Fry on <u>low</u> heat until egg is done – do not over cook!

My Tips for mineral reduced canned Salmon:

_____

_____

_____

_____

_____

_____

_____

_____

_____

_____

_____

_____

_____

_____

_____

_____

SALMON
(Fresh – fillets)

Approximate mineral concentration per 100 grams (about 3 ½ ounces) **before** demineralizing:

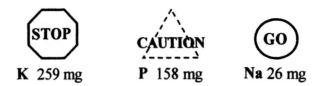

| **K** 259 mg | **P** 158 mg | **Na** 26 mg |

How to Mineral Reduce this Food

Author's note – Salmon must be cut into strips of ½ inch thickness (or less) in order to demineralize properly. Salmon can be cut easily when it is slightly frosty.

Step one: Place salmon slices in a sieve and rinse *gently* for 10 to 15 seconds under warm tap water (approximately 100°F). Allow meat to drip out in a sieve before proceeding to step two.

Step two: Place salmon slices in warm water (approximately 100°F) for 30 minutes. Warm water demineralization is carried out in a thoroughly clean bowl, outside the refrigerator. Be sure to use a 1 quart minimum volume per ½ pound of fish.

Step three: Empty the bowl into a thoroughly clean sieve, and rinse the meat for 10 to 15 seconds under cold running tap water to cool the fish. Place strips in cold tap water (same volume as before) in the refrigerator for 8 hour. At the end of the demineralization time, drain, then remove excess moisture by placing between a small stack of paper towels and pressing gently. Use immediately, or store the fish in a clean container, in the refrigerator, if you plan to cook the meat later the same day. If you plan to cook the meat another day, freeze demineralized meat immediately. For food safety considerations, use non-frozen demineralized meat within 24 hours.

Optimal Processing Time: 8 Hours and 30 Minutes

Approximate mineral concentration per 100 grams (about 3 ½ ounces) **after** demineralizing:

| GO | GO | GO |
| **K** 11 mg | **P** 61 mg | **Na** <5 mg |

Approximate mineral reduction potential **after** demineralizing:
| 96% | 61% | 85% |

126

My Tips for mineral reduced Salmon fillets:

SHRIMP
(Cooked & frozen – cocktail or popcorn size)

Approximate mineral concentration per 100 grams (about 3 ½ ounces) **before** demineralizing:

GO	STOP	STOP
K 26 mg	P 249 mg	Na 398 mg

How to Mineral Reduce this Food

Author's Note – Seafood spoils *rapidly* if left at room temperature or above. Be sure to thaw only the amount desired at the time you intend to mineral-reduce it.

Step one: Remove **frozen** shrimp from the bag. Place in a bowl of warm (approximately 100°F) or hot (>100°F) water. Alternately rub and gently squeeze the shrimp with your fingers to remove any ice chunks and encourage rapid thawing. Thawing should be complete in 1 to 2 minutes. Once thawed, empty contents into a sieve and rinse under warm tap water (approximately 100°F) for about 30 seconds.

Step two: Place shrimp in cold tap water for 30 minutes Use about 2 quarts of water per 40 – 50 small shrimp. Place the bowl in the refrigerator for the duration of the time.

Step three: Pour shrimp into a sieve and rinse for at least 30 seconds with **cold** tap water. Place between several paper towels and press gently to remove the maximum amount of moisture.

Optimal Processing Time: 30 Minutes

Approximate mineral concentration per 100 grams (about 3 ½ ounces) **after** demineralizing:

GO	CAUTION	CAUTION
K 21 mg	P 134 mg	Na 197 mg

Approximate mineral reduction potential **after** demineralizing:
19%	46%	51%

My Tips for mineral reduced Shrimp:

_____

_____

_____

_____

_____

_____

_____

_____

_____

_____

_____

_____

_____

_____

_____

_____

_____

_____

_____

_____

_____

_____

_____

_____

SPAM
(Processed - canned meat)

Approximate mineral concentration per 100 grams (about 3 ½ ounces) **before** demineralizing:

STOP   CAUTION   STOP

K 260 mg   **P** 130 mg   **Na** 1390 mg

How to Mineral Reduce this Food

Author's Note – Spam is an especially greasy canned meat. Because of this, demineralization process is less efficient. Nevertheless, a 5 minute boil will have significant impact on the final mineral value.

Step one: Remove the Spam from the can and cut into slices about ¼ inch in thickness. Rinse Spam for approximately 30 seconds under warm tap water (approximately 100ºF). Drain in a sieve.

Step two: Place Spam directly into boiling water, 2 quarts per can of Spam. You will notice a grease layer forming on the surface of the water. Boil for approximately 5 minutes.

Step three: Remove Spam from the boiling water, place in **cold** water to cool. Drain thoroughly. Place Spam slices between a small stack of paper towels and pat gently to remove excess moisture.

Optimal Processing Time: Approximately 5 Minutes

Approximate mineral concentration per 100 grams (about 3 ½ ounces) **after** demineralizing:

CAUTION   GO   STOP

K 146 mg   **P** 89 mg   **Na** 606 mg

Approximate mineral reduction potential **after** demineralizing:
44%   **32%**   **56%**

My Tips for mineral reduced Spam:

TUNA
(Canned meat)

Approximate mineral concentration per 100 grams (about 3 ½ ounces) **before** demineralizing:

CAUTION   GO   CAUTION

K 136 mg   P 92 mg   Na 219 mg

How to Mineral Reduce this Food

Step one: Open the can, empty contents into a sieve and break tuna into small chunks. Rinse under **warm** tap water (approximately 100ºF) for 15 to 20 seconds.

Step two: Place tuna in warm water (approximately 100ºF) for 30 minutes. Warm water demineralization is carried out in a thoroughly clean bowl outside the refrigerator. Use about 1 - 2 quarts of water per can of tuna.

Step three: At the end 30 minutes, pour contents of bowl into a sieve and rinse tuna with cold tap water to cool the fish. Place on several paper towels to remove the maximum amount of moisture.

Optimal Processing Time: 30 Minutes

Approximate mineral concentration per 100 grams (about 3 ½ ounces) **after** demineralizing:

GO   GO   GO

K 5 mg   P 51 mg   Na 9 mg

Approximate mineral reduction potential **after** demineralizing:
96%   45%   96%

*Author's note – For those of you who normally find tuna too 'strong', you will be pleasantly surprised to find that demineralized tuna has a mild flavor which does not need mayonnaise, or another condiment, to cover it up. Use mayonnaise or mustard sparingly on mineral reduced tuna.

Recipe Ideas for Tuna:

Here is a fast and delicious salad that will keep you coming back for more! Remember to demineralize **all** meat, and vegetable ingredients **before** beginning.

Tuna Salad

One can (or small pouch) of demineralized tuna;
To this add 2 TBS of finely minced onion;
1 small sweet pickle – finely minces;
1 hard boiled egg (or 3 hard boiled egg whites) – finely chopped;
2 TBS of finely minced celery;
Add mayonnaise to taste;
Mix thoroughly, chill briefly, and serve.

My Tips for mineral reduced Tuna:

_____
_____
_____
_____
_____
_____
_____
_____
_____
_____
_____
_____
_____
_____
_____

TURKEY
(Fresh - ground)

Approximate mineral concentration per 100 grams (about 3 ½ ounces) **before** demineralizing:

K 245 mg   P 208 mg

*NOTE – If your turkey has been injected with the food additive (sodium/disodium) phosphate, **see** '**A Word About...Food Additives**'. The above values are for <u>non-injected</u> meats.

How to Mineral Reduce this Food

Step one: Measure out the desired amount of ground turkey, place into a thoroughly clean sieve and rinse vigorously under warm tap water (approximately 100°F) for 1 minute.

Step two: Place one pound of ground turkey in a minimum of 2 quarts of cold tap water (or 2 pounds of ground turkey in 3 quarts). Stir for 15 – 20 seconds and allowed food to set for one hour in the refrigerator.

Step three: At the end of the mineral-reduction time, drain meat in a sieve, then remove excess moisture by balling the ground turkey in your hands and placing it on a small stack of paper towels. Blot dry.

Optimal Processing Time: 60 Minutes

Approximate mineral concentration per 100 grams (about 3 ½ ounces) **after** demineralizing:

K 45 mg   P 75 mg

Approximate mineral reduction potential **after** demineralizing:
82%   64%

My Tips for mineral reduced ground Turkey:

WALLEYE
(Fresh – fillet)

Approximate mineral concentration per 100 grams (about 3 ½ ounces) **before** demineralizing:

STOP
K 302 mg

STOP
P 238 mg

How to Mineral Reduce this Food

Author's Note – Walleye must be cut into strips of ½ inch thickness (or less) in order to demineralize properly. Walleye can be cut easily when it is slightly frosty.

Step one: Place walleye slices in a sieve and rinse *gently* for 10 to 15 seconds under warm tap water (approximately 100°F). Allow fish to drip out in a sieve before proceeding to step two.

Step two: Place walleye slices in warm water (approximately 100°F) for 30 minutes. Warm water demineralization is carried out in a thoroughly clean bowl, outside of the refrigerator. Be sure to use a 1 quart minimum volume per ½ pound of fish.

Step three: Empty the bowl into a thoroughly clean sieve, and rinse the fish for 10 to 15 seconds under cold running tap water to cool the fish. Place strips in cold tap water (same volume as before) in the refrigerator for 8 hour. At the end of the demineralization time, drain, then remove excess moisture by placing between a small stack of paper towels and pressing gently. Use immediately, or store the fish in a clean container, in the refrigerator, if you plan to cook the fish later the same day. If you plan to cook the fish another day, freeze demineralized meat immediately. For food safety considerations, use non-frozen demineralized meat within 24 hours.

Optimal Processing Time: 8 Hours and 30 Minutes

Approximate mineral concentration per 100 grams (about 3 ½ ounces) **after** demineralizing:

GO
K 20 mg

GO
P <62 mg

Approximate mineral reduction potential **after** demineralizing:
93%   **<74%**

My Tips for mineral reduced Walleye:

_____

_____

_____

_____

_____

_____

_____

_____

_____

_____

_____

_____

_____

_____

_____

_____

_____

_____

_____

_____

_____

_____

VEGETABLES

Vegetables – Take Note

As a rule, the only mineral you must be concerned about in vegetables is potassium. However, there are a few notable exceptions where phosphorus comes into the picture, such as in the mushroom, parsnip, and potato – just to name a few. Sodium excess is only seen in canned products, where it is added during processing.

There are also vegetables that can not be properly demineralized when raw, such as peas, corn, mushrooms, and okra. In general, canned vegetables demineralized better and faster then their raw counterparts.

Vegetables Tested

Artichokes hearts

Asparagus

Green beans

Beets

Broccoli

Cabbage (red)

Carrots

Celery

Corn

Garlic

Lettuce

Mushroom

Okra

Onion

Parsnips

Peas

Peppers

Potato (fresh [generic and Yukon Gold] and dry – flake)

Potato (sweet potato)

Pumpkin

Sauerkraut

Spinach

Squash (summer – Zucchini)

Squash (winter- Butternut)

Tomato (fresh and canned)

ARTICHOK HEARTS

(Canned)

Approximate mineral concentration per 100 grams (about 3 ½ ounces) **before** demineralizing:

K 90 mg

How to Mineral Reduce this Food

Author's note - While canned artichoke is a modest potassium food, this author has found that there are usually strong 'can', and citric acid, tastes due to this additive. Demineralization processing of this food will greatly reduce these undesired tastes as well.

Step one: Empty the contents of a can into a sieve and rinse for about 30 seconds under warm tap water (approximately 100°F) then allow them to drain briefly.

Step two: Place artichoke hearts in a minimum water volume of one small can (about 1 cup vegetable matter), to one quart warm tap water (approximately 100°F) stir gently to disperse, and allowed food to stand for one hour on the counter

Step three: After mineral reduction process has been completed, drain in a kitchen sieve.

Optimal Processing Time: 60 Minutes

Approximate mineral concentration per 100 grams (about 3 ½ ounces) **after** demineralizing:

K 51 mg

Approximate mineral reduction potential **after** demineralizing:
43%

142

Tips for: Artichoke Hearts

Artichoke hearts are a great addition to any homemade, demineralized pizza. They are also great as a stand-alone vegetable, or a garnishment for meats. Artichoke hearts have a very mild flavor that won't overpower anything they are cooked with.

My Tips for mineral reduced Artichoke hearts:

_____

_____

_____

_____

_____

_____

_____

_____

_____

_____

_____

_____

_____

_____

_____

_____

_____

ASPAGAGUS
(Fresh)

Approximate mineral concentration per 100 grams (about 3 ½ ounces) **before** demineralizing:

K 207 mg

How to Mineral Reduce this Food

Step one: Clean spears thoroughly. Remove dirt, and any old, discolored vegetable matter. Cut slices of uniform thickness (approximately ¼") then rinse under warm tap water (approximately100°F) and drain briefly.

Step two: Place asparagus slices in a minimum of 4 times its volume of warm tap water (approximately 100°F). Examples of such 4-fold excess would mean combining: 1 cup of food material and 4 cups of water, or, 1 liter of food material and 4 liters of water in a large mixing bowl. Stir briefly and allow food to set for one hour on the counter.

Step three: After one hour, drain the contents in a sieve, refill the container with fresh **cold** tap water (same volume), return asparagus to the container, stir vigorously to disperse, then allow food to set until the end of the second hour.

Optimal Processing Time: 2 Hours

Approximate mineral concentration per 100 grams (about 3 ½ ounces) **after** demineralizing:

K 148 mg

Approximate mineral reduction potential **after** demineralizing:
27%

Tips and Recipe Ideas for: Asparagus

Try asparagus with mushrooms, peas or carrots for a mixed vegetable dish.

White asparagus is never as strong tasting as green.

My Tips for mineral reduced Asparagus:

_____

_____

_____

_____

_____

_____

_____

_____

_____

_____

_____

_____

_____

_____

_____

_____

GREEN BEANS
(Canned)

Approximate mineral concentration per 100 grams (about ¾ cup) **before** demineralizing:

K 68 mg   Na 262 mg

How to Mineral Reduce this Food

Note -- Demineralization is not necessary if you purchase a *no salt added* green been product. However, you may still want to give any *no salt added* product a brief 30 minute mineral reduction processing in order to remove the "*can*" taste that is usually present in a canned product.

Step one: Empty the contents of a can into a sieve, rinse for about 15 seconds under warm tap water (approximately 100°F), now allow beans to drain briefly. This step aids in removing salt which is added by the manufacturer.

Step two: Place beans in 4 times the volume (minimum of 1 quart per small can [about 1 cup] of beans) of warm tap water (approximately 100°F). Stir briefly, now allow food to set for one hour on the counter.

Step three: Drain beans into a kitchen sieve.

Optimal Processing Time: 60 Minutes

Approximate mineral concentration per 100 grams (about 3 ½ ounces) **after** demineralizing:

K 13 mg   Na 48 mg

Approximate mineral reduction potential **after** demineralizing:
80%   **81%**

My Tips for mineral reduced Green Beans:

BEETS
(Canned)

Approximate mineral concentration per 100 grams (about ¾ of a cup or 3.5 ounces) **before** demineralizing:

△
CAUTION

K 162 mg

How to Mineral Reduce this Food

Author' note – Raw beets are too difficult to demineralize effectively.

Step one: Empty the contents of a can into a sieve, rinse for about 30 seconds under warm tap water (approximately 100ºF), allow to drain briefly.

Step two: Place beets in 4 times the volume (minimum of one quart per medium can) of warm tap water (approximately 100ºF). Stir briefly, now allow food to set for one hour, on the counter

Step three: Drain beets into a kitchen sieve.

Optimal Processing Time: 60 Minutes

Approximate mineral concentration per 100 grams (about 3 ½ ounces) **after** demineralizing:

(GO)

K 52 mg

Approximate mineral reduction potential **after** demineralizing:
68%

My Tips for mineral reduced Beets:

BROCCOLI
(Fresh)

Approximate mineral concentration per 100 grams (about 2/3cup, or 3 ½ ounces) **before** demineralizing:

STOP

K 300 mg

How to Mineral Reduce this Food

Author's Note - Reduce broccoli floret clusters to a size of 1" or less in diameter for optimal mineral reduction impact.

Step one: Cut and then rinse florets for about 30 seconds under warm tap water (approximately 100°F), allow to drain briefly.

Step two: Place florets in 4 times the volume (minimum of one quart per medium can) of warm tap water (approximately 100°F). Stir briefly, now allow food to set for one hour, on the counter. After one hour has been completed, drain into a kitchen sieve.

Step three: Refill container with fresh cold tap water (same volume). Return the food to the container, stir vigorously for 15 – 20 seconds, and allow food to set, in the refrigerator, until the end of the demineralization period. It is not necessary to change the water.

Step four: After demineralization has been completed, drain into a kitchen sieve.

Optimal Processing Time: 8 Hours *

Approximate mineral concentration per 100 grams (about 3 ½ ounces) **after** demineralizing:

CAUTION

K 185 mg

Approximate mineral reduction potential **after** demineralizing:
38%

Tips and Recipe Ideas for: Broccoli

* Alternately, broccoli can be allowed to demineralize in the refrigerator overnight without loss of taste.

If broccoli is to be used raw in a cold salad or with a dip, be sure to remove as much of the water as possible. This is best accomplished by allowing florets to drain on several paper towels for at least one hour before use.

If broccoli is to be cooked, remove the florets directly from the last demineralization bath and place them in fresh water for cooking. Do not use any water, which has been used for demineralization to cook in.

Author's note – Greater mineral reduction for broccoli can be achieved if all of the water used to cook the broccoli in is discarded after cooking.

Broccoli and Cheese

This is a simple time tested old standby that tastes great demineralized.

Drizzle warm melted (demineralized) Swiss cheese over the top of cooked broccoli and serve with no-trans-fat margarine.

My Tips for mineral reduced Broccoli:

_____

_____

_____

_____

_____

_____

_____

_____

_____

CABBAGE - RED
(Fresh)

Approximate mineral concentration per 100 grams (about 1 ½ cups or 3.5 ounces) **before** demineralizing:

STOP

K 219 mg

How to Mineral Reduce this Food

Author's note – Cabbage leaves must be cut into thin ribbons or shredded in order to demineralize.

Step one: Wash or rinse cabbage before use to remove dirt, and bug spray. Remove all old outer leaves before cutting. Cut cabbage head in half. Crosscut the base to a depth of one to two inches. Pass the cut end over a kitchen slicer, or slice the shredded end with a long knife. The end product should be thick ribbons of cabbage. Rinse shreds before proceeding to the next step.
Alternately, place chunks of cabbage, with an equal amount of water, in a blender. Run *briefly* on slow speed until the desired shredded consistency is achieved. Empty water and continue to Step two.

Step two: Place shredded or ground cabbage in 4 times the volume (minimum of one quart per medium can) of warm tap water (approximately 100°F). Stir briefly, now allow food to set for one hour, on the counter.

Step three: After one hour has been completed, drain into a kitchen sieve

Optimal Processing Time: 60 Minutes *

Approximate mineral concentration per 100 grams (about 3 ½ ounces) **after** demineralizing:

GO

K 76 mg

Approximate mineral reduction potential **after** demineralizing:
65%

Tips and Recipe Ideas for: Cabbage – red

* Cabbage can be allowed to demineralize in the refrigerator overnight without loss of taste.

Author's note – Cabbage allowed to demineralize and additional 7 hours will loose only approximately 10% more of its potassium content.

If cabbage is to be used raw, as coleslaw, be sure to remove as much of the water as possible. This is best accomplished by placing cabbage in several paper towels and squeezing it gently.

If shredded cabbage is to be cooked, place it in fresh water for cooking. Do not use any water, which has been used for demineralization to cook in.

Cabbage and Beef

Slowly simmer cabbage and beef together until done. Now drain and serve – either as is or with melted cheese.

My Tips for mineral reduced Cabbage:

_____

_____

_____

_____

_____

_____

_____

_____

_____

_____

_____

CARROTS
(Fresh)

Approximate mineral concentration per 100 grams (about ¾ of a cup or 3.5 ounces) **before** demineralizing:

STOP

K 391 mg

How to Mineral Reduce this Food

Step one: Wash or rinse carrots before cutting. Cut into slivers or for better results, cut into 1/8 to ¼ inch chunks. Rinse briefly.

**Alternately, carrots can be shredded in a blender by placing chunks of carrots, with an equal amount of water, in a blender. Run *briefly* on slow speed until the desired shredded consistency is achieved. Empty water and continue to Step two.

Step two: Place carrots in 4 times the volume (minimum of 1 quart) of warm tap water (approximately 100°F). Stir briefly, now allow food to set for one hour, on the counter. At the end of the hour, drain the warm water, refill with cold tap water, place in the refrigerator.

Step three: Because the recommended demineralization time is overnight (16 hours) , be sure to change the water once before going to bed.

Discard all the water used for demineralization before cooking!

Optimal Processing Time: 16 Hours *

Approximate mineral concentration per 100 grams (about 3 ½ ounces) **after** demineralizing:

CAUTION

K 177 mg

Approximate mineral reduction potential **after** demineralizing:
55%

154

Tips and Recipe Ideas for: Carrots

*Raw carrots are *very* difficult to demineralize, even when slivered or cut into small chunks. Greater mineral loss occurs when carrots are shredded. Cooking demineralized carrots, followed by discarding the water, will also increase mineral loss.

Carrots etc..

Here is yet another carrot recipe.

To ½ pound of cooked and drained, and finely diced baby carrots, add:
  ¼ pound of finely diced parsnips,
  Finely chopped parsley to taste,
  A shake of onion powder,
  A TSP of margarine.
Now add 1 – 2 TBS of cooked and ground leftover hamburger;
A short squirt of ketchup.

Simmer together briefly – until hot – now add honey or sugar to taste.
Serve hot.

My Tips for mineral reduced Carrots:

———————————————————————————
———————————————————————————
———————————————————————————
———————————————————————————
———————————————————————————
———————————————————————————
———————————————————————————
———————————————————————————
———————————————————————————

CELERY
(Fresh)

Approximate mineral concentration per 100 grams (about one large stalk or 3.5 ounces) **before** demineralizing:

STOP

K 316 mg

How to Mineral Reduce this Food

Author's note – For this book, celery was treated as if it were the final product and were going to be used raw in a dip. Significantly more mineral reduction could be obtained if the celery were sliced thinly, in a cross-wise fashion, demineralized, then cooked and the water discarded.

It is important that you use *only* fresh celery, without withered, yellowed, or rot spotted areas on the stalk.

Step one: Remove outer leaves and wash celery stalks. Cut lengthwise into 3 or 4 pieces.

Step two: Place celery in 4 times the volume (minimum of one quart) of warm tap water (approximately 100°F). Allow food to set for one hour, on the counter.

Step three: At the end of the hour, drain the warm water, refill with cold tap water, place in the refrigerator. Celery can be left in water, in the refrigerator, for at least a week, and some mineral reduction will continue to occur throughout the entire time. If you plan to do this, be sure to change the water daily.

Optimal Processing Time: At least 60 Minutes

Approximate mineral concentration per 100 grams (about one large stalk or 3.5 ounces) **after** demineralizing:

STOP

K 239 mg

Approximate mineral reduction potential **after** demineralizing:
24%

Tips for: Celery

Celery makes an excellent 'paddle' for holding dips of all kinds. Finely chopped celery is a great addition to soups, salads, and meat dishes. Use your imagination - demineralized celery is as versatile as you want it to be.

My Tips for mineral reduced Celery:

_____

_____

_____

_____

_____

_____

_____

_____

_____

_____

_____

_____

_____

_____

_____

_____

_____

_____

_____

_____

CORN
(Canned – sweet corn)

Approximate mineral concentration per 100 grams (about ½ cup or 3.5 ounces) **before** demineralizing:

CAUTION   GO   CAUTION

K 112 mg   P 38 mg   Na 149 mg

How to Mineral Reduce this Food

Step one: Empty the contents of a can into a sieve, rinse for about 30 seconds under warm tap water (approximately 100°F), allow to drain briefly.

Step two: Place corn in 4 times the volume (minimum of one quart per 10 - 16 ounce can) of warm tap water (approximately 100°F). Stir briefly, now allow food to set for one hour, on the counter.

Step three: Drain corn into a kitchen sieve.

Optimal Processing Time: 60 Minutes

Approximate mineral concentration per 100 grams (about ½ cup or 3.5 ounces) **after** demineralizing:

GO   GO   GO

K 59 mg   P 24 mg   Na 81 mg

Approximate mineral reduction potential **after** demineralizing:
47%   37%   46%

Note – For information on the impact demineralization had on the carbohydrate content of corn, see – **'A Word About ... Carbohydrates and Amino Acid Composition'.**

Tips for: Corn (canned sweet corn)

This favorite mainstay is always 'in season' for any meal. Corn is a great fill-in for hundreds of dishes as well as being a stand-alone dish. Here are a few suggestions for your demineralized vegetable:

Corn (as a side dish)   Corn (as part of a vegetable stuffing mix)
Corn and peas   Corn and carrots
Corn and onions   Corn and mixed vegetables
Corn and mashed potatoes   Corn and ham
Corn and beef   Corn and any poultry
Corn and any game meat   Corn in any casserole
Corn in a meat pie   Corn and cheese dish

Let your imagination run wild!

My Tips for mineral reduced Corn:

_____

_____

_____

_____

_____

_____

_____

_____

_____

_____

_____

_____

GARLIC
(Fresh)

Approximate mineral concentration per 100 grams (about one large whole bulb or 3.5 ounces) **before** demineralizing:

STOP

K 479 mg

How to Mineral Reduce this Food

Author's note – One small to medium size clove of garlic has been reported to contain approximately 12 mg of potassium. The potassium content of a single clove of garlic is too low to be concerned about.

Step one: Peel the garlic bulb and individual cloves. Using a sharp paring knife, slice cloves into thin slices (about 1/8 inch thickness). Rinse slices briefly.

Step two: Place slices in 4 times the volume (minimum of two quarts per whole bulb sliced or minimum of on quart for any lesser amount of garlic) of warm tap water (approximately 100°F). Stir briefly, now allowed garlic to set for one hour, on the counter top. **

Step three: Drain garlic. You may wish to remove extra moisture by placing garlic slices on a small stack of paper towels.

Optimal Processing Time: 60 Minutes

Approximate mineral concentration per 100 grams (about 3.5 ounces) **after** demineralizing:

STOP

K 286 mg

Approximate mineral reduction potential **after** demineralizing:
40%

160

Tips for: Garlic

** Soaking finely sliced garlic increases it's pungent qualities *dramatically*! Seasoning with a small amount of demineralized garlic can very effectively replace a large quantity of undemineralized garlic in a recipe.

Attention Garlic Lovers

Never underestimate the *raw power* of demineralized garlic!

There is a rather funny story connected with an incident at the laboratory responsible for assaying the demineralized garlic for this book. Send me an Email at: WLJ_1998@yahoo.com and I will share it with you.

My Tips for mineral reduced Garlic:

_____
_____
_____
_____
_____
_____
_____
_____
_____
_____
_____
_____
_____
_____

LETTUCE
(Fresh head lettuce)

Approximate mineral concentration per 100 grams (about 1 ½ cups of coarsely shredded or 3.5 ounces) **before** demineralizing:

△ CAUTION

K 129 mg

How to Mineral Reduce this Food

Note -- Lettuce is not normally considered a high potassium food, however if you regularly experienced indigestion after eating lettuce, demineralizing it may help to alleviate the problem. This author has personally found that to be the case.

Lettuce leaves must be cut or shredded in order to demineralize.

Step one: Remove outer leaves and rinse before using. Cut or shred the desired number of leaves. Rinse shreds before proceeding to the next step.

Step two: Place shredded leaves in 4 times the volume (minimum of one quart minimum) of warm tap water (approximately 100°F). Stir gently and allow lettuce to set for one hour, on the counter.

Step three: After one hour has been completed, drain in a kitchen sieve. Replace with cold water, and place in the refrigerator for a second hour. At the end of the second hour, drain lettuce in a sieve or colander. Use as soon as possible for maximum freshness.

Optimal Processing Time: 2 Hours

Approximate mineral concentration per 100 grams (about 1 ½ cups or 3.5 ounces) **after** demineralizing:

(GO)

K 54 mg

Approximate mineral reduction potential **after** demineralizing:
58%

Tips for: Lettuce (head lettuce)

Not all lettuce is suitable for demineralization processing. Some of the leaf varieties are too tender to withstand this treatment. Both head and Romaine lettuce can be demineralized.

My Tips for mineral reduced Lettuce:

_____
_____
_____
_____
_____
_____
_____
_____
_____
_____
_____
_____
_____
_____
_____
_____
_____
_____

MUSHROOMS
(Canned – button type)

Approximate mineral concentration per 100 grams (about 2/3 cup or 3.5 ounces) **before** demineralizing:

CAUTION   GO   STOP

K 112 mg   P 44 mg   Na 292 mg

How to Mineral Reduce this Food

Step one: Empty the contents of a can into a sieve, rinse for about 30 seconds under warm tap water (approximately 100°F), allow to drain briefly.

Step two: Place mushrooms in 4 times the volume (about one quart per 4-6 ounce can) of warm tap water (approximately 100°F). Stir briefly, now allow food to set for one hour, on the counter.

Step three: Drain mushrooms in a kitchen sieve.

Optimal Processing Time: 60 Minutes

Approximate mineral concentration per 100 grams (about 2/3 cup or 3 ½ ounces) **after** demineralizing:

GO   GO   GO

K 28 mg   P 40 mg   Na 91 mg

Approximate mineral reduction potential **after** demineralizing:
75%   **9%**   **69%**

Tips for: Mushrooms (canned)

If mushrooms are to be used in a dry salad, blot excess moisture off on a couple of paper towels before using. If they are to be cooked in liquid, proceed directly to your favorite recipe without blotting.

Though it is not necessary, mushrooms can be demineralized for a second hour using cold tap water. Mineral reduction will continue, reducing all three target minerals (approximately) an additional 10%.

Mushrooms are a great low-calorie filler in hamburger dishes, as well as with scrambled eggs, mixed vegetable dishes, and in soups.

My Tips for mineral reduced Mushrooms:

_____

_____

_____

_____

_____

_____

_____

_____

_____

_____

_____

_____

_____

_____

_____

_____

_____

OKRA
(Canned)

Approximate mineral concentration per 100 grams (about 2/3 cup or 3.5 ounces) **before** demineralizing:

GO	GO	STOP
K 52 mg	P 13 mg	Na 356 mg

How to Mineral Reduce this Food

Step one: Empty the contents of a can into a sieve, rinse for at least 60 seconds under warm tap water (approximately 100°F), allow to drain briefly. This treatment will remove a great deal of the citric acid that is added by the manufacturer to preserve color.

Step two: Place okra in 4 times the volume (about one quart per 10 – 16 ounce can) of warm tap water (approximately 100°F). Stir briskly, now allow food to set for one hour, on the counter.

Step three: Drain in a kitchen sieve at the end of the mineral reduction period.

Optimal Processing Time: 60 Minutes

Approximate mineral concentration per 100 grams (about 2/3 cup or 3.5 ounces) **after** demineralizing:

GO	GO	CAUTION
K 29 mg	P 10 mg	Na 201 mg

Approximate mineral reduction potential **after** demineralizing:
44%	23%	44%

Recipe Ideas for: Okra (canned)

Here are two hot okra meals that are sure to wake up the taste buds. Leftovers are just the natural evolution of a great meal -- make plenty -- okra dishes are great the second time around!

Okra Dish Delight (all materials used are demineralized **before** being used in these dishes)
Ingredients:
1 (14 ounce) can of diced tomatoes
1 medium can of whole kernel corn
2 (14-15 ounce) cans of okra
1 large onion finely diced
8 slices of bacon (real or fake)
1 TBS of sugar
1 TBS ketchup
1 TBS BBQ sauce (optional -- only if you want a certain flavor)
¼ tsp of liquid smoke (optional)
2 -- 3 TBS of no-trans-fat-margarine

Put margarine in a pan and sauté the onions -- add tomatoes and corn while cooking;
Add Okra and bacon and continue to cook until all ingredients have blended.

Fried Okra (Use demineralized Okra)
1 to 2 cans (14-15 ounce) of okra
Flour
Cornmeal
No-trans-fat-margarine

Be sure there is a thin layer of no-trans-fat-margarine melted in the pan;

Mix 1:1 cornmeal and flour -- place in a bag -- now add dried okra and shake;

With a large slotted spoon, sift out the okra and place in a hot skillet and do not crowd it.

Okra fries better when there is a little space between neighbors;

Fry on medium-high heat, turning frequently -- okra will tend to absorb oil so be sure to keep more no-trans-fat-margarine available;

Remove from heat when lightly brown on all sides.

You may wish to turn the okra out into a paper towel lined bowl to absorb any extra oil that clings.

ONION
(Fresh – white, commercial bulb type)

Approximate mineral concentration per 100 grams (about one small bulb, 1/3 of a large bulb, or 3.5 ounces) **before** demineralizing:

K 55 mg

How to Mineral Reduce this Food

Author's note – The bulb onion is not normally a high potassium food, however if you regularly experienced indigestion after eating this food, demineralizing it may help to alleviate the problem. This author has had problems with onions, and has personally found that the problem disappears when onions are demineralized.

Onions must be cut into thin rings in order to demineralize.

Step one: Remove dry outer peels and rinse before using. Slice into thin rings, preferably using a vegetable slicer, or cut into 1/8 inch thick rings with a knife. Rinse rings under warm water (approximately 100°F) before proceeding to the next step.

Step two: Place rings in 4 times the volume (minimum of two quarts per medium size onion) of warm tap water (approximately 100°F). Stir gently and allow rings to set for one hour, on the counter.

Step three: After one hour has been completed, drain in a kitchen sieve. Place rings on a paper towel to remove moisture, then store in a container 'lined' with a paper towel, in the refrigerator to catch residual moisture.

Optimal Processing Time: 60 Minutes

Approximate mineral concentration per 100 grams (about 3.5 ounces) **after** demineralizing:

K 35 mg

Approximate mineral reduction potential **after** demineralizing:
36%

Tips for: Onion

Onions can be demineralized for a second hour. While this will not reduce the potassium load more than a few percentage points, it does reduce the tendency of the onion to upset the stomachs of those sensitive people.

Remember, if you choose to do a second hour demineralization, refill with cold water, and place in the refrigerator for the second hour. At the end of the second hour, drain in a sieve or colander. Use as soon as possible for maximum crispness.

Onions are milder after demineralization, so plan to use them in dishes you may not normally use onions. They also make great onion rings, fried or simmered onions, and can even be eaten as-is in a tossed salad.

My Tips for mineral reduced Onion:

_____
_____
_____
_____
_____
_____
_____
_____
_____
_____
_____
_____
_____
_____
_____

PARSNIPS
(Fresh)

Approximate mineral concentration per 100 grams (about ½ to ¾ cup or 3 ½ ounces) **before** demineralizing:

STOP

K 569 mg

CAUTION

P 121 mg

How to Mineral Reduce this Food

Step one: Wash and peel parsnips. Cut into ¼ inch pieces with a knife or slice thinner with a kitchen slicer. Rinse slices.

Step two: Bring water to a boil and add slices. Wait until water resumes boiling, then boil slices *at least* 5 minutes.

Author's note - Parsnip may require a longer cooking time to reach the degree of doneness you desire. Boil parsnips until done (but at least 5 minutes).

Step three: Drain parsnips carefully when finished. Vegetable is now somewhat fragile and can break up.

Optimal Processing Time: A rolling boil for at least 5 Minutes

Approximate mineral concentration per 100 grams (about ½ to ¾ cup or 3.5 ounces) **after** demineralizing:

GO

K >9 mg

GO

P 56 mg

Approximate mineral reduction potential **after** demineralizing:
>98%   54%

Tips for: Parsnip (fresh)

Parsnips are much milder after demineralization. Use parsnips with carrots, peas, and onions for a great tasting mixed vegetable dish.

My Tips for mineral reduced Parsnips:

_____
_____
_____
_____
_____
_____
_____
_____
_____
_____
_____
_____
_____
_____
_____
_____
_____
_____
_____

PEAS
(Canned)

Approximate mineral concentration per 100 grams (about 2/3 cup or 3 ½ ounces) **before** demineralizing:

CAUTION   GO   STOP

K 105 mg   **P** 84 mg   **Na** 286 mg

How to Mineral Reduce this Food

Step one: Empty the contents of a can (10- 16 ounce can) into a sieve, rinse for about 30 seconds under warm tap water (approximately 100°F), allow to drain briefly.

Step two: Place peas in 4 times the volume (about one quart per can) of warm tap water (approximately 100°F). Stir briefly, now allow food to set for one hour, on the counter.

Step three: Drain peas in a kitchen sieve.

Optimal Processing Time: 60 Minutes *

Approximate mineral concentration per 100 grams (about 2/3 cup or 3 ½ ounces) **after** demineralizing:

GO   GO   GO

K 33 mg   **P** 71 mg   **Na** 113 mg

Approximate mineral reduction potential **after** demineralizing:
69%   15%   60%

*Author's note – Peas can be demineralized for 2 hours with no loss in taste. The second hour is a cold water demineralization. At the end of the second hour, the approximate mineral values should be:

GO   GO   GO

K 13 mg   **P** 66 mg   **Na** 41 mg
Approximate mineral reduction potential **after** demineralizing:
88%   21%   86%

Tips for: Peas

If peas are to be used in a dry salad, blot excess moisture off on a couple of paper towels before using. If they are to be cooked in liquid, proceed directly to your favorite recipe without blotting.

There are as many uses for peas as there are with corn. For information on how the demineralization process impacts the carbohydrate content of peas, see - **'A Word About ...Carbohydrates and Amino Acid Composition'.**

My Tips for mineral reduced Peas:

_____

_____

_____

_____

_____

_____

_____

_____

_____

_____

_____

_____

_____

_____

_____

_____

_____

PEPPER
(Fresh - green)

Approximate mineral concentration per 100 grams (about 3.5 ounces) **before** demineralizing:

K 161 mg

How to Mineral Reduce this Food

Step one: Rinse peppers to remove bug spray and dirt before cutting. Cut into rings with a kitchen slicer or knife. For best results, cut into 1/8 to ¼ inch thickness. Rinse briefly.

Step two: Place pepper rings in 4 times the volume (minimum of one quart per two large peppers) of warm tap water (approximately 100°F). Stir briefly, now allow food to set for one hour, on the counter. At the end of the hour, drain the warm water, refill with cold tap water, place in the refrigerator.

Step three: Because the recommended demineralization time is 8 hours (7 hours in cold water), be sure to change the cold water once during the cycle. If you plan to leave peppers demineralize overnight, be sure to change the water once before going to bed.

Optimal Processing Time: 8 Hours

Approximate mineral concentration per 100 grams (about 3.5 ounces) **after** demineralizing:

K 82 mg

Approximate mineral reduction potential **after** demineralizing:
49%

Tips for: Peppers (fresh - green)

Peppers: Did you know – Fun Facts

The nutritional value of any pepper changes with its stage of maturity, and varies greatly from soil type to soil type.

Any pepper is a good source of vitamin A and C, however the red ones have greater amounts of these vitamins.

Red peppers are an especially good source of beta-carotene.

Coating your hands with stiff or thick fat can help prevent skin 'burns' when working with very hot peppers varieties.

Read more about peppers and get pepper recipes at:

http://whatscookingamerica.net/SweetPepperRecipes.htm

http://www.urbanext.uiuc.edu/veggies/peppers1.html

My Tips for mineral reduced Peppers:

_____

_____

_____

_____

_____

_____

_____

_____

_____

_____

POTATO
(Dry potato flakes)

Approximate mineral concentration per 100 grams (about one to 1.5 cups dry or 3.5 ounces) **before** demineralizing:

K 1047 mg   **P** 124 mg

How to Mineral Reduce this Food

Author's note — 1/3 cup of dried potato flakes makes approximately 2/3 of a cup prepared mashed potatoes (depending upon the brand used), and more closely approximates a serving size.

Step one: Measure out the desired quantity of potato flakes. Use two quarts of warm tap water (approximately 100°F) for every cup of flakes. Stir and allow food to set for one hour on the counter.

Step two: At the end of the hour, drain the warm water by pouring *slowly* into a small mesh sieve. Alternately, the sieve can be lined with a paper towel to catch the first flakes (See 'Tips'). Let potato flakes remain in the sieve to drain until they stop dripping.

Step three: Transfer demineralized potato flakes onto a stack of paper towels and allow it to dry further. Alternately, you can ball the flakes in a paper towel and squeeze gently to remove maximum moisture.

Optimal Processing Time: 60 Minutes

Approximate mineral concentration per 100 grams (about 3 ½ ounces) **after** demineralizing:

K 42 mg   **P** 20 mg

Approximate mineral reduction potential **after** demineralizing:
96%   84%

Note — An additional 2% loss of potassium is possible after a second hour of demineralization

Tips and Recipe Ideas for: Potato (flakes)

Potato flakes will swell about 1.5 X during demineralization, making it less likely (though not impossible) that they will pass through a small mesh sieve. As you start to pour, you will notice that some of the first flakes will pass through the sieve. In order to prevent this, place a large bowl under the sieve or colander to catch potato flakes that initially pass through. As you pour slowly you will notice that the swollen flakes will begin to 'wedge' in the mesh until the potato flakes no longer pass through the holes.

Alternately, a sieve can be lined with a paper towel to catch the first flakes. This is a must when working with Potato Buds.

For information on how the demineralization process impacts the carbohydrate content of potato (flakes), see - **'A Word About ...Carbohydrates and Amino Acid Composition'**.

Potato Soup (all materials are demineralized **before** use)

Ingredients:
2 cups of potato flakes
1 large onion (finely diced)
1 pound of hamburger
2 cloves of garlic (finely minces)
sage, poultry seasoning
No-trans-fat- margarine

Slowly cook the meat in margarine with the onions, garlic, and seasoning until the meat is done and the tastes have melded together. Now add 2 cups of water and continue to simmer for a minute or two before adding the mash potatoes. Be sure to mix thoroughly. This dish can stand on the stove on 'low' heat for 30 minutes to bring out the subtleties of the seasoning.

POTATO
(Fresh –generic)

Approximate mineral concentration per 100 grams (one small potato or about 3.5 ounces) **before** demineralizing:

K 395 mg

How to Mineral Reduce this Food

Step one: Peel then rinse all potatoes before slicing. Slice potatoes as finely as possible. This can best be achieved by using a kitchen slicer. Otherwise slice potatoes to a thickness no greater than ¼ inch.

Author's note - Maximum potassium reduction can only be achieved if potato slices are no thicker than 1/8". Potatoes that are sliced or diced at a thickness of ½ inch **will not** demineralize properly.

Step two: Rinse sliced potatoes thoroughly before proceeding. For every pound of potatoes use **approximately** two quarts of warm tap water (approximately 100°F). Stir to distribute potato slices then allow to set for one hour on the counter.

Step three: Drain in a sieve. Add fresh water to potatoes and boil until done, then drain all water before mashing, or use for frying.

Optimal Processing Time: 60 Minutes + boiling time *

Approximate mineral concentration per 100 grams (about ½ to ¾ cup or 3.5 ounces) **after** demineralizing **and boiling:**

K 54 mg

Approximate mineral reduction potential **after** demineralizing:
86%

Tips and Recipe Ideas for: Potatoes (fresh - generic)

- Potatoes can be demineralized overnight in the refrigerator.
  The potassium loss observed was as follows, after:
  Warm tap water (approx.100°F)   for: **1 Hour – K** 252 mg (36%) ◯ *stop*

  Cold tap water for: **2nd Hour – K** 234 mg (41%) ◯ *stop*

  4rd Hour – K 231 mg (42%) ◯ *stop*

  8th Hour – K 222 mg (44%) ◯ *stop*

  16th Hour – K 219 mg (46%) ◯ *stop*

Demineralized raw potatoes must be boiled and the water discarded to achieve maximum mineral reduction.

Scalloped Potatoes (all vegetable ingredients are demineralized before use)
Ingredients:
1 ½ pound of potatoes (thoroughly demineralized through the boil step)
2 medium onions (diced)
2 TBS margarine
2 TBS of flour
¼ TSP of black pepper
1/8 TSP paprika
1 ½ cup of liquid non-fat dry milk **(NOTE – this is a high phosphorus and potassium item!)**
1 TBS parley
No-trans-fat- margarine

Cook potatoes and onion together in a no-trans-fat- margarine oiled pan until both are completely done. Stir milk, flour, pepper, paprika and cook until thick and smooth. Layer 1/3 of the potatoes and onions in a lightly greased pan – sprinkle ½ of the parsley and 1/3 of the sauce on top – repeat till thoroughly layered concluding with the sauce on top. Bake at 400°F uncovered for about 35 minutes until lightly golden brown and tender.

Demineralized cheese or ham can be added for extra 'body'.

POTATO – YUKON GOLD
(Fresh)

Approximate mineral concentration per 100 grams (about one small potato or 3.5 ounces) **before** demineralizing:

K 398 mg   P 53 mg

Author's note – A dietitian in Calgary Canada informed me that, *"...not all potatoes were created equal...Yukon Gold was definitely different."* From the demineralization data that we collected, I would tend to agree. The Yukon Gold potatoes we worked with demineralized better and easier then our generic potatoes tested.**

How to Mineral Reduce this Food

Step one: Peel then rinse all Yukon Gold potatoes before slicing. Slice potatoes as finely as possible. This can best be achieved by using a kitchen slicer. Otherwise slice potatoes to a thickness no greater than ¼ inch.

Author's note - Maximum potassium reduction can only be achieved if potato slices are no thicker than 1/8". Potatoes that are sliced or diced at a thickness of ½ inch **will not** demineralize properly.

Step two: Rinse sliced potatoes thoroughly before proceeding. For every pound of potatoes use *approximately* two quarts of warm tap water (approximately 100°F). Stir to distribute potato slices then allow to set for one hour on the counter.

Step three: Drain in a sieve. Place in a cook pot, add fresh water, simmer or boil (for a minimum of **2 minutes**) until done, then drain all water before mashing, or use for frying.

Optimal Processing Time: 60 Minutes + 15 minutes simmer

Approximate mineral concentration per 100 grams (about ½ to ¾ cup of mashed potato or 3.5 ounces) **after** demineralizing:

K 22 mg   P 30 mg

Approximate mineral reduction potential **after** demineralizing:
94%   **45%**

Tips for: Yukon Gold Potato

- Potatoes can be demineralized overnight in the refrigerator.
  The potassium loss observed was as follows, after:
  Warm tap water (approx.100°F)   for: **1 Hour** – K 203 mg (49%) ⬡ *stop*

  Cold tap water for: 7 additional **Hours** – K 164 mg (59%) △ *caution*

Demineralized raw potatoes must be boiled and the water discarded to achieve the maximum final mineral reduction. (go)

My Tips for mineral reduced Potatoes (Yukon Gold):

_____

_____

_____

_____

_____

_____

_____

_____

_____

_____

**Do you agree with the dietitian from Calgary Canada – that the Yukon Gold potato is a cut above the rest ? Send me an e-mail and give me your thoughts on this 'sporty spud'.

POTATO
(SWEET POTATO)
(Fresh)

Approximate mineral concentration per 100 grams (about 2/3 cup or 3.5 ounces) **before** demineralizing:

K 244 mg

How to Mineral Reduce this Food

Step one: Peel then rinse before slicing. Slice potatoes as finely as possible. This can best be achieved by using a kitchen slicer. Otherwise slice potatoes to a thickness no greater than ¼ inch.

Author's note - Maximum potassium reduction can only be achieved if potato slices are no thicker than 1/8". Potatoes that are sliced or diced at a thickness of ½ inch **will not** demineralize properly.

Step two: Rinse sliced potatoes thoroughly before proceeding. For every pound of potatoes use *approximately* two quarts of warm tap water (approximately 100°F). Stir to distribute potato slices then allow to set for one hour on the counter.

Step three: Drain in a sieve. Replace with cold water – same volume, and let set in the refrigerator **at least** 8 hours, or overnight (see '**Tips**').

Optimal Processing Time: At least 8 Hours*

Approximate mineral concentration per 100 grams (about 2/3 cup or 3.5 ounces) **after** demineralizing:

K 198 mg*

Approximate mineral reduction potential **after** demineralizing:
19%

Tips for: Sweet Potato

Am I eating a Sweet Potato or a Yam?

A visit to your favorite grocery store may leave you wondering. In one isle a can is prominently labeled '**yam**' with '*sweet potato*' in fine print, while in the fresh produce section, '**sweet potato/yam**' may be displayed over the same bumpy looking plant matter. With people seemingly using the two words interchangeable, you may begin to wonder if it isn't simply a case of, "*You say potato and I'll say pototo.*" The answer is – No, there is a difference. Unless you have trekked to one of those specialty stores, it is virtually 99.9% certain that you are eating a Sweet Potato. The word 'Yam' is an English form of the African word '*nyami*' which actually refers to an edible root from the *Dioscorea* genus of plants. The reason you frequently see both words together is that, because they tend to be interchangeable used in the U.S.A., the U.S. Department of Agriculture requires that the label "yam" always be accompanied by "sweet potato." For a detailed description of both, go to: http://aggie-horticulture.tamu.edu/plantanswers/vegetables/sweetpotato.html - several good recipe ideas can be found on that web page as well.

- Though not done for this book, it is likely that the sweet potato will demineralize to the same or similar degree, seen with either of the aforementioned fresh potatoes, after boiling. Demineralized raw potatoes must be boiled and the water discarded to achieve the maximum final mineral reduction potential.

Author's note - The reason an overnight demineralization was recommended is because it was discovered that the sweet potatoes, used to generate this data, actually tasted *sweeter* after being let to demineralize overnight.

PUMPKIN
(Fresh)

Approximate mineral concentration per 100 grams (about 2/3 cup or about 3.5 ounces) **before** demineralizing:

```
 _____
/      \
| STOP |
_____/
```

K >680 mg

How to Mineral Reduce this Food

Step one: Peel pumpkin before slicing into thin strips.

Author's notes – The pumpkin flesh will peel away from the hard shell easier if it is cut into large chunks and microwaved until it is very warm (or hot) to the touch. You may have to experiment with the time a little, but this 'pre-treatment' makes peeling a lot easier.

Because pumpkin is course and tough in texture, it may not be possible to slice them uniformly thin unless you are using a vegetable slicer or put them in the blender for a brief shot (see **'Tips'** for blender information). Try to slice pumpkin into strips of less than ½ inch. Remember the thicker the slices the less efficient will be your demineralization treatment. Canned pumpkin **can not** be demineralized at all.

Step two: Rinse strips before proceeding. For every pound of pumpkin strips, use *approximately* two quarts of warm tap water (approximately 100°F). Stir to distribute slices then allow to set for one hour on the counter.

Step three: Drain in a sieve. Place in boiling water – boil for a *minimum* of **5 minutes** (longer if you desire), then drain completely (see 'Tips').

Optimal Processing Time: 60 Minutes + 5 Minute Boil

Approximate mineral concentration per 100 grams (about 2/3 cup or about 3.5 ounces) **after** demineralizing:

```
   /\
  /  \
 /CAUTION\
 --------
```

K <113 mg

Approximate mineral reduction potential **after** demineralizing:
>83%

Tips for: Pumpkin

Blender Processing

Since pumpkin pie/pudding recipes all call for cooked and mashed pumpkin, an easier alternative to slicing strips of pumpkin for demineralization, is to simply chunk up the peeled pumpkin into a blender. Be sure to fill the blender equally with pumpkin and water (50/50) and observe the manufacturers recommended maximum filling capacity. A short run/bursts should reduce the pumpkin to shreds, which should demineralize easier. Once shredded, processed the pumpkin through the 60 minutes warm water bath, drain, place in boiling water and boil 5 minute. Finally, drain and mash.

Author's note – While no data was generated on blender shredded pumpkin, this author believes it is likely that the mineral removal efficiency is greater for pumpkin treated in this manner

Are you counting calories – why not try pumpkin pudding instead of pie!

How you ask?

Simple!

Take your favorite pumpkin recipe and just 'tweak it' to remove (or reduce) the sugar, and proceed through the cooking stage. Once cooked, refrigerate in a bowl and use like a pudding. You will be cutting out the calories of the pie shell.

SAUERKRAUT
(Canned)

Approximate mineral concentration per 100 grams (about 1/3 cup of juiceless sauerkraut) **before** demineralizing:

CAUTION

K 170 mg

STOP

Na 520 mg

How to Mineral Reduce this Food

Step one: Open can (or package) and drain contents in a sieve.

Step two: Submerge sauerkraut in warm tap water (approximately 100°F) for 5 minutes.

Author's note - For a more robust tasting sauerkraut, this author suggested that you only *rinse* with warm tap water (approximately 100°F) for 1 minute. However, there is no demineralization data available for this short period.

Step three: Allow sauerkraut to drain in the sieve. Alternately sauerkraut can be pressed or placed on a paper towel to remove more moisture. This is especially important if the sauerkraut will be used in a sandwich or as part of a 'dry' dish.

Optimal Processing Time: 5 Minutes

Approximate mineral concentration per 100 grams (about 1/3 cup of juiceless sauerkraut) **after** demineralizing:

GO

K 24 mg

GO

Na (Not detected)

Approximate mineral reduction potential **after** demineralizing:
86%   **>99%**

Tips and Recipe Ideas for: Sauerkraut

Demineralized sauerkraut can be used in both hot and cold dishes as well as in a wide variety of recipes. The following are a few suggestions:

Ketchup 'N' Kraut on a Bun

Try spicing up your demineralized hotdog sandwich with a little demineralized sauerkraut and ketchup mix.

Krazy Krauter Relish

Ingredients:

        1/2 cup vinegar

        1/4 to 1/3 cup of white sugar

        1/2 teaspoon of mustard (any kind)

        1/8 to 1/4 teaspoon (or to taste) of garlic powder

        8 to 12 ounces of demineralized sauerkraut

        1/4 to 1/3 cup of chopped sweet pepper

(for added color try mixing green, yellow, and red sweet pepper)

        1/4 cup of chopped cucumber

        1/4 cup (or to taste) of chopped onion

Use a mixing bowl large enough to contain a 4-cup volume. Thoroughly mix the vinegar, sugar, mustard, garlic powder, and pepper. Stir in sauerkraut, cucumbers and onions. Cover the bowl and place in the refrigerator for a minimum of 2 hours before using. Makes between 2 ½ to 3 cups of relish, which can be stored in the refrigerator 4 to 5 days.

My Tips for mineral reduced Sauerkraut:

_____

_____

_____

_____

_____

_____

SPINACH
(Canned)

Approximate mineral concentration per 100 grams (about 3.5 ounces) **before** demineralizing:

K 128 mg

P 16 mg

How to Mineral Reduce this Food

Step one: Open the spinach can and drain contents in a sieve. Rinse briefly under warm tap water (approximately 100°F).

Step two: Place spinach in sauce pan (or microwaveable container) and cover with an excess of water. Bring spinach to a boil and simmer for 2 minutes.

Step three: Drain all water away before serving.

Optimal Processing Time: 2 Minutes

Approximate mineral concentration per 100 grams (about 3.5 ounces) **after** demineralizing:

(GO)

K 21 mg

(GO)

P 12 mg

Approximate mineral reduction potential **after** demineralizing:
84%   **25%**

Tips for: Spinach

My Tips for mineral reduced Spinach:

_____

_____

_____

_____

_____

_____

_____

_____

_____

_____

_____

_____

_____

_____

_____

_____

_____

_____

_____

_____

_____

_____

_____

_____

SQUASH
(Zucchini)
(Fresh)

Approximate mineral concentration per 100 grams (about ½ cup or 3.5 ounces) **before** demineralizing:

K 211 mg   P 37 mg

How to Mineral Reduce this Food

Step one: Wash squash to remove dirt and bug spray before slicing (peeling is optional depending upon the maturity of the squash and your preference). Slice zucchini into uniform thickness of approximately ¼ inch.

Author's note - Use a kitchen slicer when ever possible.

Step two: Place zucchini squash slices in warm tap water (approximately 100°F – minimum of 4 times its volume), stir carefully to disburse slices, then allow food to set for one hour on the counter.

Step three: At the end of the demineralization period, drain squash. If zucchini will be used in a dry dish (e.g. a salad or as a condiment) place on a small stack of paper towels to remove excess moisture.

Optimal Processing Time: 60 Minutes

Approximate mineral concentration per 100 grams (about ½ cup or 3.5 ounces) **after** demineralizing:

K 141 mg   P 28 mg

Approximate mineral reduction potential **after** demineralizing:
33%   **24%**

Tips for: Squash (Zucchini)

Zucchini can be demineralized for up to two hours. This additional hour will reduce the potassium an additional 3%. Demineralizing longer than two hours renders the final product tasteless.

Cooking the zucchini in an excess of water then draining it will reduce the potassium further.

My Tips for mineral reduced Squash (Zucchini):

_____

_____

_____

_____

_____

_____

_____

_____

_____

_____

_____

_____

_____

_____

_____

_____

_____

SQUASH
(Butternut - winter)
(Fresh)

Approximate mineral concentration per 100 grams (about ½ cup or 3.5 ounces) **before** demineralizing:

STOP

K 323 mg

How to Mineral Reduce this Food

Step one: Peel the Butternut squash before slicing into thin strips of approximately ¼ inch..

Author's note – A thoroughly ripe Butternut squash is tough to peal and the flesh is very course, and tough textured. It may not be possible to slice this squash into uniformly strips. In order to demineralize properly, strips must be less than ½ inch thick (see '**Tips**' for an alternate procedure).

Step two: Rinse strips before proceeding. For every pound of strips, use *approximately* two quarts of warm tap water (approximately 100°F). Stir to distribute strips then allow it to set for one hour on the counter.

Step three: Drain in a sieve. Refill with cold water and place in the refrigerator for the remainder of the period. It is not necessary to change the water.

Optimal Processing Time: 8 Hours *

Approximate mineral concentration per 100 grams (about ½ cup or 3.5 ounces) **after** demineralizing:

CAUTION

K <193 mg

Approximate mineral reduction potential **after** demineralizing:
<40%

Tips and Recipe Ideas for: Squash (Butternut - winter)

* Blender Processing

Since this squash usually ends up mashed after cooking, an easier alternative to slicing strips of Butternut squash for demineralization is to simply chunk up the peeled winter squash into a blender. Be sure to fill the blender equally with squash and water (50/50) and observe the manufacturers recommended maximum filling capacity. Several short bursts should reduce the squash to shreds, which can very easily be demineralized. After shredding, process the squash through the 60 minutes warm water bath, drain, then cook to doneness in an excess of water, then drain completely. Add butter and serve.

Author's note – While no data was generated on blender shredded winter squash, this author believes it is likely that the mineral removal efficiency will be much greater.

My Tips for mineral reduced Squash (Butternut - winter):

_____
_____
_____
_____
_____
_____
_____
_____
_____
_____
_____

TOMATO
(Fresh)

Approximate mineral concentration per 100 grams (about one small tomato – 2 inches in diameter, or 3.5 ounces) **before** demineralizing:

K 208 mg

How to Mineral Reduce this Food

Step one: Wash and slice tomatoes thinly – approximately 1/8 inch thick slices. Tomatoes sliced thicker than ¼ of an inch will not demineralize properly.

Step two: Place tomato slices in a minimum of 4 times its volume (one quart minimum) of warm tap water (approximately 100°F), stir gently to disperse the slices, and then allow food to set for 1 hour on the counter top. At the end of the time, drain away warm water, refill with cold tap water and place in the refrigerator for an additional 7 hours.

Step three: Drain, and lay slices on a paper towel to remove excess water. Be sure to use to tomatoes within 24 hours.

Optimal Processing Time: 8 Hours

Approximate mineral concentration per 100 grams (about 3.5 ounces) **after** demineralizing:

K 75 mg

Approximate mineral reduction potential **after** demineralizing:
64*%

TOMATOES
(Canned)

Approximate mineral concentration per 100 grams (about ½ cup of solid, juiceless tomato flesh, or 3.5 ounces) **before** demineralizing:

K 212 mg

Na 160 mg

How to Mineral Reduce this Food

Step one: Open can and drain away the juice. If the tomatoes are whole, slice into quarters before rinsing. If the tomatoes are already slice, rinse briefly before proceeding to Step two.

Step two: Place tomato slices in a minimum of 4 times its volume (one quart minimum) of warm tap water (approximately 100°F) per can (approximately 10 to 12 ounce can). Stir gently to disperse the tomatoes, and then allow food to set for 1 hour on the counter top.

Step three: At the end of the time, drain in a sieve.

Optimal Processing Time: 60 Minutes

Approximate mineral concentration per 100 grams (about 3.5 ounces) **after** demineralizing:

GO

K 43 mg

GO

Na 54 mg

Approximate mineral reduction potential **after** demineralizing:
80%   **66%**

Tips for: Tomatoes (fresh and canned)

Demineralized tomatoes can be used in more places than this author can count. Beside their usefulness in the culinary arts there is another side of tomatoes that has caught the attention of science.

The Lycopen connection

Tomatoes have a substance called lycopenes. Lycopenes are a member of the carotenoids family. Other members of this family are found in numerous heavily colored vegetables (beta carotene – found in carrots is one example). Lycopenes are believed to be a powerful antioxidant – perhaps the most powerful one in the carotenoid family. Licopenes have been in the cancer research spotlight because increased lycopene consumption has been associated with a lower risk of prostate cancer.

Read about lycopenes and the research findings at: www.tomato.org

My Tips for mineral reduced Tomatoes:

_____

_____

_____

_____

_____

_____

_____

_____

_____

A Word About ...

A Word About – *Coffee*

Hey, what's in my cup of 'joe'?

Have you ever wondered what's lurking just under the surface of your dark cup of morning brew? Is there really anything more then just water, color, and a little something to 'jump-start' your engines (caffeine)? You may be surprised to learn that your favorite blend of coffee may contain as many as 700 different aromatic elements, all melded together. What looks like a simple hot drink, is actually a chemistry shop in your cup!

Worth the wait

The coffee bean is not chemically simple nor fresh picked. This truly amazing bean actually contains a complex array of natural substances, which include – chlorogenic acid, albumin, carbohydrates, fatty materials, as well as minerals and salts. The beans that became part of your drink today have been aged – sometimes for as long as 8 years before being roasted, then packaged – all just to bring out that unique flavor that you savor.

Bloom-O-rama

Don't think that your coffee's usefulness has come to an end with your last sip (unless of course it was instant coffee). There is a potential 'garden' of growth waiting to be unleashed in the grounds at the bottom of your pot. Because of the high nitrogen content in coffee grounds, they will make a good garden fertilizer. Coffee grounds also contain other things such as **potassium, phosphorus**, and **trace minerals**, in various concentrations, depending upon the original beans blended.

For an overview of this mysterious brew you can read:

'*Coffee: From Wikipedia, the free encyclopedia*' (http://en.wikipedia.org/wiki/Coffee)

'*All About Coffee*' www.jeremiahspick.com

Potassium, phosphorus, and trace minerals – oh my!

And herein lies the problem. Some brands of coffee contain potassium. If you are a one-cup per day person, and your potassium levels are OK, the fact that your favorite blend may contain a significant amount of potassium is probably of little concern to you. On the other

198

hand, if coffee is a beverage that you consume in large quantities, you may wish to contact the coffee company, by calling their toll-free consumer information number, to get the facts for yourself.

This author contacted the makers of Folgers and Taster's Choice. The consumer's service center reported that the brand Taster's Choice, 100% Naturally Decaffeinated Instant Coffee contained neither potassium nor phosphorus. Folgers Consumer Nutritional Data sheet listed varying amounts of potassium for their coffees, non-decaf as well as decaf (ground, instant, singles), ranging from 70.8 mg to 163.7 mg per cup.

A Word About – *Powdered Cheese and Soup Mixes*

This author checked the potassium or phosphorus content of a 25 gram sample (about 1/8"
cup), of several no-name brands of finely powdered soup mixes and cheddar cheese, which
are distributed by Frontier Natural Products, and available through some health food stores.
This amount of powder soup mix is to be added to two 6-ounce cups of water. A single
serving is therefore approximately 12.5 grams, or about one tablespoon of mix. While none of
the soup mixes contained added salt, the potassium content, of most materials tested, was
found to be high.

Mild Cheddar Cheese:

  163.7 mg of phosphorus per **two** tablespoons (about 25 grams)

  82 mg per **one** Tablespoon.

Mushroom Soup Powder:

  387.5 mg of potassium per **two** tablespoons (about 25 grams)

193 mg per **one** Tablespoon.

Tomato Powder:

  825.0 mg of potassium per **two** tablespoons (about 25 grams)

  413 mg per **one** Tablespoon.

Vegetable Soup Powder:

  272.2 mg of potassium per **two** tablespoons (about 25 grams),

193 mg per **one** Tablespoon.

A Word About – *Fats and Protein*

The demineralization process had a measurable impact on the general fat content of the foods which were tested.

Fats:

Samples of almonds and peanuts were processed in order to determine the impact demineralization has on total fat content of a food.

Unprocessed almonds: 43.5% fat content (K = 433 mg/100g & P = 546 mg/100g)
*Demineralized almonds: 27.2% fat content (K = 163 mg/100g & P = 374 mg/100g)
*Demineralization process for almonds is not listed in this book.

Unprocessed peanuts: 45.4% fat content (K = 574 mg/100g & P = 394 mg/100g)
Demineralized peanuts: 20.3% fat content (K = 301 mg/100g & P = 260 mg/100g)

Protein:

The small but measurable impact, seen on the protein content of the two meats (beef and pork) tested, is probably due to the fact that demineralization remove a good deal of residual blood from meats – a protein material.

Protein content of 100 grams of beef and pork, before and after processing for 30 minutes:

Unprocessed ground beef: 25.3% protein content
Demineralized ground beef: 22.2% protein content

Unprocessed ground pork: 19.0% protein content
Demineralized ground pork: 18.7% protein content

A Word About – *Carbohydrates and Amino Acid Composition*

Carbohydrates:

Demineralization was observed to minimally reduce the carbohydrate content of the foods tested.

Unprocessed peas:	16.7% carbohydrate content
Demineralized peas:	11.6% carbohydrate content
Unprocessed Yukon Gold Potatoes:	22.0% carbohydrate content
Demineralized Yukon Gold Potatoes:	14.9% carbohydrate content
Unprocessed corn:	15.1% carbohydrate content
Demineralized corn:	14.0% carbohydrate content

Amino Acid:

Demineralization appears to have little impact on the amino acid composition of a food. To find out the extent of the impact, control and processed samples of beef hamburger and beef liver were subjected to amino acid analysis. Of the 18 amino acids tested, only Alanine, Glutamic acid, Histidine, and Serine showed small, but consistently reduced quantities in both meats after processing. The following is general information about each of these amino acids.

Alanine is a non-essential amino acid. This means your body can make it from other branch-chain amino acids. Alanine is reported to be involved in the regulatory mechanism for blood sugar level.

Glutamic acid is also a non-essential amino acid. This amino acid is reported to be principally used in brain chemistry.

Histidine is an essential amino acid (primarily during infancy). This means your body can not make it, and it needs to be supplemented.

Serine is a nonessential amino acid that is essential for the metabolism of fats as well as fatty acids.

A Word About – *Food Additives*

Sodium Phosphates

The food additives labeled as sodium phosphate or disodium phosphate, have been creeping into our grocery store meats for some time now. In general, the sodium phosphate group (monobasic, dibasic, and tribasic) are injected into meats, as an 'X%' solution (this author has seen 10% sodium phosphate solution in beef, and up to 15% in packaged chickens), before they are packaged. According to the meat producing industry, these additives are used to retain moisture and help prevent overcooking. These phosphates have also been used as: Buffering agents, Dietary Supplements, Emulsifiers, Foaming Agent, Neutralizing Agents, Nutrients, Texture-Modifying Agents, Texturizers, and Whipping Agent. You can read more about the approved food additive list at: http://www.nutritiondata.com/food-additives.html.

Unfortunately, the sodium phosphate food additive can raise the total phosphate and sodium levels of the meat you are eating. Fortunately, the demineralization procedure for that meat can reduce the total phosphate and sodium levels, regardless of where it originally came from. The following are the test results for beef hamburger, which had been injected with up to 10% sodium phosphate solution, before processing.

Raw Beef Hamburger

	Control Beef (no additive)	Injected Beef (a sodium phosphate enhance)
Pre –demineralization	K 216 mg , P 123 mg, Na 44 mg	K 314 mg, P 271 mg, Na 232 mg
After-demineralization	K 36 mg, P 70 mg, Na 9 mg	K 32 mg, P 99 mg, Na 31mg

A Word About – *Stomach Upset*

For some people (as is the case with this author) there are certain foods that the stomach (and tongue) find too 'strong' (i.e. contain too much of substance 'X'). Most food categories have several potential offenders – tomatoes, carrots, parsnips, grapefruit, lettuce, peppers, and tuna – just to name a scant few. Through demineralization, food seems to undergo a remarkable transformation. Instead of 'shouting' its presence all the way down your throat, it tends to 'whisper', "*Here I come*". For some stomachs, this could be just what the body ordered, translating into few incidents of stomach upset.

Take tuna, for example. Some people report that the taste is so strong they having to bury it in salad dressing (or peanut butter) before it can be eaten. But such is not the case with *demineralized tuna.* Give it a try and you may agree that tuna is a food that can be enjoyed without a lot of embellishments.

A Personal Invitation

Are you someone who has been told to reduce one or more minerals in your daily diet?

Are you a renal patient?

Has mineral reducing your diet had a positive impact on your health in some way?

We want to hear about it in your own words.

You are cordially invited to share your own story for inclusion in a possible
Third edition of this book.

Compose your best 100 words (don't worry about going over -- we won't count)
and send an Email to Wendy at: **WLJ_1998@yahoo.com**

Happy demineralizing!

About The Author

Wendy Lou Jones, a former resident of Arlington Minnesota, completed her Bachelors study in biological science at Southwest State University in 1974, Masters studies at South Dakota State University in 1979, and initiated a Ph.D. studies in Calgary Canada in 1982.

A dynamic, success oriented clinical and research investigator in the fields of renal research and biotechnology, Wendy Jones has held positions in the US, Canada, and Austria – amassing more than 25 years of combined laboratory experience in oncology in Calgary Canada; at Minnesota's Mayo Clinic in immunology/arthritis and transgenic research; as medical/technical writer in one of Vienna Austria's largest pharmaceuticals; as Royal Knight's president, scientific entrepreneur, and clinical trials manager.

Her articles and stories, scientific and non-scientific, have appeared in numerous publications including the Rolex Foundation Journal, Journal of Renal Nutrition, Anti-Aging Research, SD Academy of Science, Bio-Techniques, Focus, Immunogenic, Midrange and Showcase Magazines, FASAB, HMS Press, Mother Earth News Magazine, iSeries, e-Business Quarterly, die ganz Woche (German language newspaper), and others.

As president of Royal Knight, Inc. – a company whose primary focus is carrying out and promoting renal research in the areas of renal nutrition, food demineralization, renal repair, and renal support, Wendy Jones actively supervises clinical studies, and provides direction and assistance to other companies seeking her expertise.